author: Robert Brightman

Guide to Home and Auto Care & Repair.

FIX·IT

  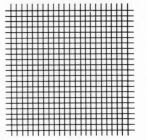

Dorison House Publishers, Inc. Cambridge/New York

This book is dedicated to my wife, Mollie, who reminded me during the writing that I had neglected some home repair jobs that needed attention.

ROBERT BRIGHTMAN was Home and Shop Editor of *Mechanix Illustrated* magazine for twenty-four years where he assigned, wrote and edited articles on all facets of home maintenance, repairs, wiring, alterations and furniture making. He also conducted a question-and-answer column on home problems called "The House Doctor." At present he writes for *Popular Mechanics, Better Homes and Gardens, McCalls,* and the *New York Times.* He is also responsible for the *Reader's Digest Complete Do-it-Yourself Manual* and for many Stanley Tools instruction booklets. He is the author of the *Home Owner's Handbook of Carpentry and Woodworking* and *Torch Tips.* He has edited nineteen books on electricity, masonry, concrete, plumbing, home repairs, heating, astronomy and photography, and has appeared on more than 100 TV and radio shows slanted to the homeowner. He is a homeowner who spends what little spare time he has keeping it shipshape.

ISBN: 0916752-18-6
Library of Congress Catalog Card Number: 77-89550
Manufactured in the United States of America

Cover & Chapter Illustrations: 19th Century engravings
Charts & drawings: Henry Clark
Book Design: Cachalot Design Group
            Marblehead, Massachusetts

CONTENTS

INTRODUCTION   5

Chapter 1 GETTING READY TO WORK.   7

Chapter 2 THE BASEMENT 33

Chapter 3 BATHROOM REPAIRS 45

Chapter 4 KITCHEN CHORES 57

Chapter 5 THE DINING ROOM 75

Chapter 6 THE LIVING ROOM 83

Chapter 7 COVERING WALLS 91

Chapter 8 ROOF WORK 105

Chapter 9 HOW TO SAFEGUARD YOUR HOME 113

Chapter 10 CAR CARE 123

Glossary of DURO Fix-It Aids 137

INDEX 141

INTRODUCTION

DURO-Woodhill is an American success story that began in 1921. Rather than have holes in his Model T Ford repaired at a professional body shop at a cost of $20 to $25, Norman J. Freeman developed a plastic auto body solder that did the job for less than 20 cents.

Word about his product got around to body shops in the Cleveland, Ohio area and orders began to come in. And since the filler was ready-to-use, the word also spread to car owners themselves.

Freeman began selling his product from a garage and called the new business The Woodhill Chemical Company. As the demand for his product increased, the company grew from a one-man and one part-time employee operation with first year sales of $6,000 (an encouraging amount in the 1920's) to a world-wide corporation with a line of 150 do-it-yourself home and automotive products carrying the DURO name.

In 1974, Woodhill Chemical was acquired by the Loctite Corporation of Newington, Connecticut. In 1977, the Permatex Company, another Loctite subsidiary, was merged into Woodhill and the company is now known as Woodhill Permatex. Loctite is the world leader in anaerobic and cyanoacrylate adhesives.

The company's success is based on four factors: 1) producing the finest quality product; 2) anticipating and recognizing consumer needs; 3) a creative approach toward meeting unmet needs; and 4) a total commitment to customer satisfaction. Woodhill Permatex works hard to achieve these goals. Employees use the latest mixing and packaging equipment and methods and an ultra-modern laboratory maintains strict quality control, from raw material to finished product.

With today's high cost of labor, the "do-it-yourself" trend for fixing things around the house or apartment is growing at a remarkable rate. As costs for professional services rise, many people are servicing and repairing their cars and boats and achieving professional results.

Look at the counters in any hardware, lumber, paint or auto supply department and you see a vast array of do-it-yourself products. You will discover after you have started the work that it is not as difficult as you had imagined. Actually, most fix-it jobs are easy, with many rewards — obtaining good results that last, experiencing creative satisfaction, personal pride in a well-maintained home, and, or course, saving money.

It is with all this in mind that we present this handy reference book for home and car care and repair. Topics covered range from the basement to the attic and from the backyard to the garage. Use the index to get to the section which covers your particular problem.

Chapter 1

GETTING READY TO WORK

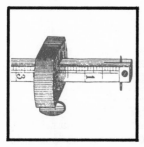

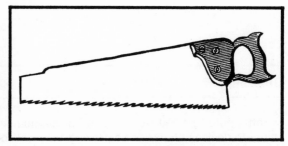

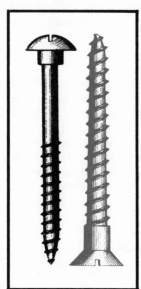

Choosing Basic Tools

Anthropologists tell us that man is distinguished from animals by his ability to devise and use tools. Having the right tools for the job is a large part of its success. If you expect to do any serious repair and maintenance work around your home, an investment in at least one tool in each of the following categories is essential.

Hammers

You should have at least one good claw hammer. Make sure it is made of forged steel, not cast iron. A second hammer similar to the claw hammer is the ripping hammer. The claw on the ripping hammer is somewhat flatter than that of the claw hammer. Since the flat claw can be used for prying, it is a handy tool for ripping up floor boards, taking boxes apart and general demolition work. A lighter hammer can be used for driving tacks, small nails and brads. Another useful hammer is the short-handled sledge, good for driving steel-cut nails into masonry and where an extra-heavy hammer blow is required.

Screwdrivers

This is the second most needed tool. Your best bet is to get a set of four, one of which should be a Phillips screwdriver. The other three should be: a "stubby" for working in close quarters; a "cabinet" screwdriver for cabinet and fine woodworking; and a general purpose screwdriver (which should *not* be used as a chisel — more about chisels later). Other screwdrivers you may want are right-angle screwdrivers, ratchet screwdrivers, tiny jeweler's screwdrivers, and push-type spiral screwdrivers.

Saws

A good hand saw is a must. There are many types but a crosscut saw (for cutting across the grain) and a hacksaw (for cutting metal) are two that you simply must have. Your crosscut should be about 26 inches long with eight teeth to the inch. Other saws that you may want are ripping saws (for cutting with the grain), a backsaw (for miter box use and fine cabinet work), a coping saw (for cutting curved shapes and openings), and a keyhole saw, to mention just a few.

Planes

These are useful tools to trim wood to an exact size and to ease sticking doors and windows. There are about ten types made but all you really need are the standard plane, (about 8 inches long), and the block plane. The latter is a handy little fellow that is used with one hand. A sort of poor relation to the plane is the *Surform.* It is a kind of glorified rasp with a handle just like a plane, and is used the same way.

Pliers

There are literally dozens of different types of pliers: round nose, *Vise-Grip,* nippers, *Channelock,* parallel jaw pliers, and many more. If you are buying only one get the kind with a slip-joint that enables the jaws to be opened extra wide for grasping large work. Another useful type is the side cutting pliers for cutting wire. These two will take care of most of the repair work around the house.

Measuring Devices

The steel tape is probably the handiest rule to have around the house. Get one that is 12 feet long and that has large, easy-to-read figures. Of course, if you want to look like a pro, get the folding zigzag ruler traditionally favored by carpenters and cabinet makers. We don't know why this ruler is still popular — most likely because steel tapes were not around when the old-time carpenters learned their trade.

Squares

This handy gadget enables you to draw lines absolutely perpendicular to a given line or surface. A square is a versatile tool — a good one combines a bubble level, an awl for marking, and a handle cut so that it can be used for laying out 45° angles. A bit up the scale is the roofing or rafter square, used by builders for laying out rafters, stairs stringers and similar parts of a house. The small square with a 12-inch leg will do for the average job.

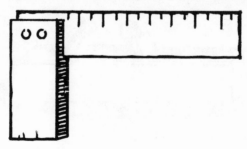

Levels

These instruments tell you if you have installed the shelves in the kitchen cabinet correctly. There are special levels for masonry work, pipe-fitting, and for general woodworking. The most generally useful is the 24-inch bubble level usually made out of cherry wood. Get one with two vials so that the level can be used for "plumbing" vertical work as well as for horizontal work.

Chisels

Handy for chiseling out the recess in a door when installing hinges and locks, and for cleaning out the wood between two parallel saw cuts. A set of three — 1/4-inch, 1/2-inch and 3/4-inch — will make a good investment. Buy the best you can afford. Cheap tools are more costly in the long run.

A Miter Box

The only way you can cut molding and framing at exact 45° angles is by means of a troughlike box which guides the saw. The miter box in combination with its backsaw will also assure you of exact perpendicular and 45° cuts. A worthwhile investment, or make your own. (See page 28.)

The Awl

Probably the least expensive tool you can buy is an awl, used for marking wood and starting screws in soft wood. Get the kind with a flat side on one side of the handle so it will not roll.

A Drill

The least expensive drilling device you can get for making holes is the hand drill, but for only a few dollars more you can get an electric drill. If you decide to spring for the electric drill, buy the kind that will accept 3/8-inch bits. And get a set of bits (from 1/16-inch to 3/8-inch in diameter). An even better bet — and well worth the extra cost — are high-speed drills. These drill bits will hold their cutting edge much longer than carbon-steel drill bits.

Wrenches

To grip and turn the head of a bolt, a nut, a pipe or such, a set of open-end wrenches, or an adjustable wrench, as well as a pipe wrench (the *Stillson*) should complete your set of tools.

Fastening Devices

There are four commonly used methods for fastening items to each other, to another part, or to a surface: nails, screws, bolts, and adhesives. We have excluded welding and riveting as their application is not very common.

Nails

There are dozens of different types of nails. The length of a nail is designated by inches and by "penny" size. This term originally referred to the price per hundred. The larger the nail the more pennies it cost to buy a hundred nails, but now it only signifies length. The chart shows the relationship of penny size to inch size. For example, a ten-penny nail is 3 inches long.

The diameter of a nail increases with its length — except for special purpose nails such as floor nails and shingle nails. In addition, nails are distinguished by their heads, a large flat head such as on the common nail and a small head — slightly wider than the shank diameter — on a finishing nail. Large-head nails hold best because the load is distributed over a larger area, but the small head is easier to conceal by driving it slightly below the surface of the wood with a nail set and covering the nail hole with putty. Another advantage of the small-head brad or finishing nail is that it can be drawn through molding and trim without marring the surface when it is necessary to disassemble a cabinet.

As a general rule, nails should be driven through the thinner piece of wood and then into the thicker piece when joining two pieces of wood. At least two-thirds of a nail should be in the thicker piece. For maximum holding power, drive the nails at a slight angle, slanting alternately towards each other and away. This way, they cannot be pulled out without bending. If you can "clinch" the nails by pounding down the tips so much the better, but you will need longer nails, long enough to pass completely through the work with at least 1/2-inch of nail protruding.

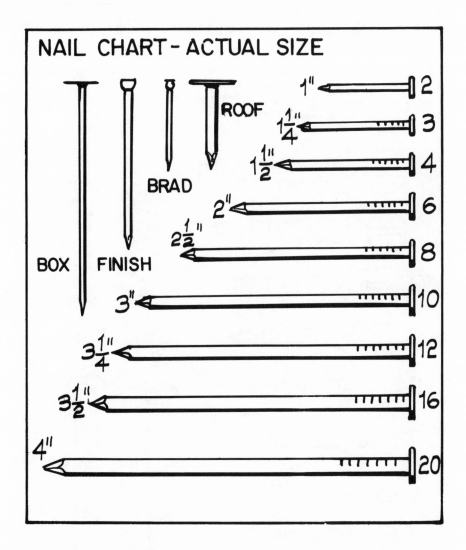

NAIL CHART – ACTUAL SIZE

ROOF

BRAD

BOX   FINISH

1" — 2
1¼" — 3
1½" — 4
2" — 6
2½" — 8
3" — 10
3¼" — 12
3½" — 16
4" — 20

Screws

Screws are a much more sophisticated fastener for joining than nails. Screws are also used when greater holding power is required and also when disassembly is a factor. The most common screw is the one with the single slot across its head. The Phillips-type screw has a second cross slot, both slightly rounded, and requires a special screwdriver. Phillips screws reduce the danger of the screwdriver slipping from the recess and possibly marring the work.

SCREW CHART – ACTUAL SIZE

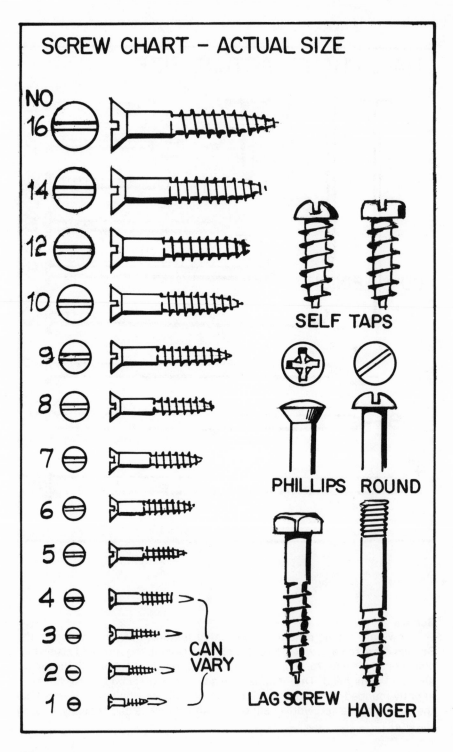

NO
16

14

12

10

9

8

7

6

5

4

3

2

1

CAN VARY

SELF TAPS

PHILLIPS   ROUND

LAG SCREW   HANGER

Screws are sold by length, diameter, head type, and of course by metal content (steel, stainless, bronze, or brass) and plating (cadmium, zinc, chromium or other metal). The length of a screw is measured in inches while the shank diameter is indicated by a number, ranging from 1 to 24. The greater the number, the thicker the diameter of the screw (see chart). The most commonly used screws around the house range from No. 6 to No. 10. The three most common heads on screws are the oval head, the flathead, and the roundhead. Roundhead and oval heads are used when the appearance of the screw head is not objectionable, while flatheads are used when some concealment is required.

Small screws can be started by making a "pilot hole" (starting hole) with an awl. Larger screws however, should always have a predrilled pilot hole. When using large screws, and especially when working with hardwood, a pilot hole as well as a clearance hole for the shank will be required. To avoid repetitive changing of bits you can get a set of drills called Screw-Mates which will drill a pilot hole, a clearance hole, and even a countersink for a flathead screw, all in one operation. This is a great timesaver when a number of screws of the same size must be driven.

When driving screws into hardwood, lubricate the screw threads with wax (soap tends to rust the threads). Washers are sometimes used under screw heads to provide extra bearing surface and to prevent marring the work when removal is required for access to inner parts such as in a hi-fi cabinet.

Real elegance when using screws is obtained by the use of plugs. These are cylinders of hardwood, driven into floors for example, to hide screw heads. The technique is to "counterbore" (deepen the hole) for the screw head, (about 1/2-inch is sufficient), and then to tap the plug into the counterbored hole. Plugs are easily cut, sometimes out of matching wood — or even out of contrasting wood — with an inexpensive device called a plug cutter mounted in a drill press. Plugs can be removed by drilling out the center and then collapsing the sides with a narrow chisel.

Bolts

The most common fastening device after nails and screws are bolts. Bolts are designated by diameter in inches and by the number of threads per inch. (Bolts also include lag bolts, Molly bolts, Jack nuts, U bolts, J bolts, and eye bolts, turnbuckles and toggle bolts.) For example, a 1/4 × 20 bolt means that it is 1/4-inch in diameter and that it has 20 threads per inch. And of course its third dimension is its length. Bolt sizes range from 1/8 × 40 to 1/2 × 13 and from 1/4-inch in length to 6 inches. Larger sizes, used in construction and industry are seldom stocked by hardware stores.

When using a bolt with wood, always use a washer under the nut to prevent the nut from digging into the wood. Use lock washers to prevent loosening and/or a chemical thread locker like Lock It™, to bond threads, especially on parts subject to vibration.

Adhesives

And now we come to a most important segment of the "fastening field" — Adhesives. Modern adhesives are so strong, reliable and durable that they are actually used in house construction in place of nails to secure subfloors to the joints. Furthermore, quite often it is impossible, and even undesirable, to fasten items together with visible nails, screws, or bolts. We must then turn to adhesives. Let us look at some of these many products.

White Glue

This is a popular glue for the workshop and for use around the house. Its chief drawback is that it is not waterproof, only water-resistant. It is usually not used for outdoor work or for joining materials subject to dampness. Excessive glue can be wiped off with a damp cloth before it sets.

Only moderate pressure should be used to secure the joint while the glue is drying; it will set in about four hours and when dry the glue is clear. White glue is not suitable for materials such as glass, metal and plastics. While it can be used for gluing paper, leather, cloth and wood, a better product for gluing fabric is Darn® fabric mender, a product especially made for such use.

Epoxies

These "glues" cure by a chemical reaction between the two "components." They are suitable for bonding hard materials such as glass, ceramics, and metals, and they can also be used in woodworking. They are usually formulated so that an equal amount of the resin must be added to the hardener. Some epoxies dry clear, while others dry white or gray. The curing or hardening time can be overnight or 5 minutes or less, depending on the epoxy. (This time can be speeded up if necessary by subjecting the joined parts to heat.)

Epoxies are among the strongest adhesives. They are available in tubes, cans and even in ribbon form, such as E-Pox-E® Ribbon. The latter comes in lengths that are each colored differently. To use, two identical lengths are snipped or torn off, and rolled between the hands until the resulting color is uniform. At this point, it will start to harden and can be used to fill gaps and mend leaks in plumbing. When it is dry, it can be sanded, drilled and filed the same as metal. Before setting it can be tooled and sculpted so as to repair carved work.

Other types of epoxies are steel-filled and one is made especially for repairing concrete.

Contact Cements

Contact cement is the adhesive to use when it is impossible to use clamps and most undesirable to use nails or other fastening means. Among its many applications is its use for bonding decorative laminates Formica and Micarta to countertops, walls, and tables. It can also be used to bond metal, hardboard and plastics to wood. However, contact cement should not be used on a painted surface as it will lift the paint, adversely affecting the bond. Furniture joints are best left to conventional adhesives.

To use, apply the cement by brush to both of the surfaces to be joined. It's best to use an old brush and discard it afterwards. (Cleaning the brush is too time-consuming and furthermore, the brush should not be used to apply paint no matter how well cleaned.) Surfaces to be joined should be clean — no grease, wax, dirt, paint or moisture. Allow the cement to dry for 10 to 15 minutes, or until the surfaces are no longer tacky.

The work to be joined must be accurately positioned, as once contact is made it is very difficult to move the pieces. A good way to assure accurate placement is to use a "slip sheet." (See page 32.)

Contact cement can also be applied with a roller and even with a spray gun, though a brush is best for home use.

It is possible — though slow work — to separate contact-cemented panels. This is done by gently prying them apart and pouring a solvent into the gap. Keep prying. Use a wedge to keep the panels apart and at the same time keep adding more solvent. A tedious procedure, but it works. Make sure you do this operation in a well-ventilated room as the fumes of the solvent — and the contact cement — are flammable.

A gallon of contact cement will bond about 250 square feet. When dry, it is resistant to heat, moisture, and oil. About 90% of its full strength develops after 24 hours of setting time.

Safe Contact Cement

This cement is water-based and can be used where a fire hazard may exist. It has most of the properties of regular contact cement. Its chief difference, besides its non-flamability, is that drying time before bonding is somewhat long, about 40 minutes or until the cement has dried clear. A second application may be necessary when used on porous surfaces such as open-grained wood.

The technique for application is the same as for the regular contact cement. Excess cement, before it has dried, can be cleaned up with warm, soapy water. However, after the cement has dried, a lacquer thinner must be used for clean-up. Its coverage is slightly greater than regular contact cement, about 10% more per container.

One great advantage of Safe Contact Cement is that it can be used over painted or varnished surfaces, provided the paint or varnish does not show any sign of flaking or poor adhesion.

Instant Adhesives

Developed to meet some rather tough demands in industry, this type of adhesive has become available to the consumer in recent years. It is based on a chemical called "cyanoacrylate," and has remarkable qualities.

Super Glue® -3 cyanoacrylate adhesive does not require any mixing or heating; it bonds permanently in seconds; the bond resists temperature, oils and most chemicals. It has a tensile strength of up to 5,000 pounds per square inch (in fact, only a single drop should be applied to each square inch on bonding surface).

It will bond to any non-porous surface such as metal, ceramic, rubber and most plastics, but it should not be used on porous surfaces such as woods, cloth or leather. Do not use this glue to fill spaces in poorly fitting joints.

To use this remarkable product, a few precautions should be observed. Surfaces should be clean and dry, free of grease or moisture. Apply only a single drop to each square inch of surface — no more. Spread the drop out so that it will cover the area to be joined. The glue should be applied to one surface only, *not both*. As soon as the glue has been applied, *immediately* bring the second surface in contact with the first. Press them together; clamping is not necessary. Keep the surfaces in good contact with each other for 20 seconds or so by which time the bond will have been made. It is best to put the work aside as the full strength of the bond is not realized until 2 hours have passed.

Some tips: clean the surfaces to be joined with nail polish remover before applying the glue. If slightly irregular, smooth with fine sandpaper first. (*Note:* too much sanding causes non-mating surfaces. This means bond failure.) A thin application of Super Glue-3 is much stronger than a heavy one. Also, the more quickly the two surfaces are joined, the stronger the bond. The better the fit between the surfaces to be joined, the better the bond.

One precaution is in order when using this adhesive. Be careful not to get it on your fingers as it will bond the skin together. If it does, don't panic. Apply some nail polish remover or acetone to the glued area, keep wet for about 1/2 minute, then gently roll or pry the skin apart.

More Glues and Cements

Animal Glues

These glues are also called hide glues. They are organic glues made from the hide, bones and sinews of cattle. Animal glues come in a powder form and are mixed with water for use. For best results they should be applied when hot. Liquid animal glues, ready to use at room temperatures are also available. They develop their strength by cooling and drying. These glues have fairly good strength but tend to become brittle as they age. They are used chiefly in furniture making and veneering.

Gums and Pastes

Rubber cement, flour paste, and vegetable glues come under this category. They are used chiefly for light work such as gluing paper, cloth, cardboard, and leather. These glues, except for rubber cement, have poor water resistance and low strength. The best glues for working with cloth, cardboard, and leather are either Darn or a household cement.

Mastics

These are heavy-bodied adhesives used for bonding ceiling tiles, floor tiles, and plywood wall panels to studs. There are two types made: synthetic latex — a water-based adhesive — and the rubber resin type which is made of synthetic rubber dissolved in a solvent. Both types bond well to concrete, hardboard, wood, and to ceramic tiles. These products are available in tubes for "gun" application and in gallon cans. Excess cement can be removed with a damp cloth, but once the cement has hardened, a rag moistened with paint thinner must be used.

Silicone Sealants

These are cream-like sealing compounds used around bathtubs and auto windshields. Early compounds would not accept paint, but they are now formulated so they can be painted.

They are available in black, white, clear, blue and "aluminum." They all have a characteristic vinegar-like odor and cure by exposure to moisture in the air. They have good bonding strength and are resistant to extremes of temperature after curing.

Waterproof Glues

For outdoor work, such as patio furniture and boat-building, a waterproof glue is an absolute must. Resorcinol is a powdered catalyst that is mixed with a liquid resin. This glue can be used with wood, concrete, laminates, and with ceramics. After thorough mixing both surfaces are coated and clamped until the glue has set. Temperature has a pronounced effect on drying time. For example, at 70°, the curing or drying time is about 10 hours. It is longer at higher temperatures and shorter at lower temperatures. Parts which are under strain should have the curing time extended. Excess glue can be removed with warm water — but only before the glue has dried.

Water-resistant Glues

A typical water-resistant glue consists of a plastic resin which is mixed with water. The usual formula calls for 5 parts of resin to 2 parts of water by volume. It is mixed to a creamy consistency and only as much glue as is needed is mixed at one time as it has a limited "pot" life. A thin coat is applied to each surface and the work must be clamped until the glue sets. The brush can be cleaned with warm water immediately after use.

These glues are recommended for use with wood, porous, and semi-porous materials, of non-mineral construction. It is also used for bonding Formica and Micarta to countertops, though contact cement is preferred for such applications. The glue is unaffected by oil, gasoline and most solvents. Though highly water-resistant, this kind of glue is not absolutely waterproof.

Hot Melt Glues

These glues can be used inside or outside the home, and require a special "heating gun," which melts the adhesive and prepares it for use. It is rubber based and water-resistant. This glue sets quickly as it cools but parts cannot be moved for adjustment. It has fairly moderate strength; no clamping is required. It can be used on wood, leather and some plastics, but is not recommended for metals, ceramics or other highly glazed and non-porous surfaces.

Adhesives For Wallpaper

There are two types made. One is the conventional wheat powder paste which is mixed with water and is used for hanging wallpaper and lightweight vinyl wall coverings. A second type is used for hanging the heavy vinyl wall coverings which are sometimes made in 54-inch widths instead of the usual 27-inch widths. This latter type is a heavy-bodied paste that must be applied with a trowel instead of a brush as can be done with the wheat paste.

Cellulose Adhesives

These adhesives are characterized by their banana-like odor. They are packaged in small squeeze tubes for mending crockery, most plastics, paper and for light metal work. Their drying time is about 3 hours, but maximum strength is achieved after overnight drying. They are resistant to water, alcohol, grease and acids. Excess cement can be cleaned away with nail polish remover or acetone.

Glues For Wood

There are three basic types of wood glues: PVA, waterproof and hot melt. Epoxy can also be used on wood. PVA (polyvinyl alcohol) wood glue has a water base. It is really white glue, modified to work specifically on wood. It is easy to use and safe. Just squeeze it directly onto a broken joint or into a loose rung on a chair. Clamp and wait. Bond will be achieved in 15 to 30 minutes. PVA is not recommended for outdoor use, as the bond would be affected by humidity.

Waterproof glue (mentioned on page 20) is used by professional furniture assemblers and woodworkers. It is resorcinol based and can withstand humidity, so it can be used for outdoor work.

Hot melt glue is described on page 21, and can be used on woods, as can epoxy glues.

There is another very large class of industrial type adhesives that have applications around the home. Called "solvent evaporation adhesives," they cure due to the elimination of a solvent, and the forming of a dry film. They are specially designed, and often specifically named, for a particular job.

Typical of this group are such products as liquid steel, plastic aluminum, weatherstrip cement, liquid solder, plastic rubber, and others.

These adhesives are ready to use right from their containers. Evaluate the job you are doing, and choose a product accordingly.

Sandpaper and Sanding Tools

No matter how painstaking you are in painting, varnishing, or any kind of operation that requires subsequent finishing, it is the preparation *prior* to finishing that will determine the appearance of the final finish. And in order to do a good sanding job, it helps to know something about sandpaper and sanding tools.

Actually the word "sandpaper" is a catchall for many types of abrasives mounted on paper and cloth. The grades of sandpaper range from very coarse to very fine. The oldest grading system uses grit symbols. The coarsest is called 4-1/4 and the finest is labeled, 10/0. The more modern system uses numbers which represent the openings per inch in a screen through which the abrasive grains can pass. These numbers range from No. 12, very coarse, to No. 600, very fine.

Modern, coated abrasives include silicon carbide (the hardest and sharpest), aluminum oxide, garnet, flint and emery. They may be mounted on paper or on cloth; may have the grains close together or far apart; may be used dry or while wet. The least expensive sandpaper is flint, a natural quartz material of a light tan color, it clogs quickly, but because of its low cost can be discarded after a few minutes of use. This is a good paper to use for cutting down painted surfaces or pitch-loaded boards.

Clean, fresh wood is best sanded with garnet paper, which is also an inexpensive material. But if you have a power sander, use aluminum oxide paper; it costs more than garnet or flint, but lasts longer and is less expensive in the long run. Silicone carbide is used for work on metals and plastics, while for polishing metal, emery is the usual choice.

Despite all the grades and types of sandpaper available, sticking to the five described below will take care of 99% of your requirements.

Very Fine
Use this grade for sanding between coats of paint, varnish and lacquer. It yields an extra smooth finish and can be used wet for metal and dry for other surfaces.

Fine
Use this grade as a final sanding before the first coat of primer or sealer. Also used on metal to remove light rust and imperfections.

Medium

Use this for light stock removal — wood or paint — power or hand sanding. Also used on walls prior to painting or papering, and for removing rust stains on metal.

Coarse

For rough stock removal, chiefly used with power belt sanders; it will smooth out deep scratches and similar imperfections before sanding with medium grade sandpapers.

Extra Coarse

Used for removing heavy coats of paint and varnish, especially from floors, nearly always used with a power sander belt or disc; also suitable for removing heavy rust deposits. Extra coarse sanding must always be followed by finer grades of paper to smooth the scars made by this paper.

All sanding should be parallel to the grain of the wood. Before starting to sand with the next finer grade of paper, wipe away the dust left by the preceeding coarser grade. And before starting to paint, varnish, shellac, or lacquer, wipe the work thoroughly with a rag or tack cloth dampened with the solvent of the material you are going to apply. This serves to remove all dust and also gives the finish a better bite.

Sandpaper is sold in packages containing three or four sheets (depending upon the grade of paper in the package). A good investment is a few tools for holding the sandpaper to make sanding easier. Get a flexible sander that will conform to the shape of the work to be sanded; a sanding kit for sanding flat surfaces; and a disc holder for use with any electric drills. Such accessories, as well as sandpaper, sandpaper discs, and aluminum oxide paper are especially packaged for home and auto repair work.

Splices and Joints

Now that we have learned something about tools, fastening devices and sandpaper, let us take a look at the many types of joints that we should know. Materials can be joined together in several ways, using nails, screws, bolts, glues or wedges as the fastening medium.

Splices

A splice connects two lengths of wood, end-to-end, so as to run in the same line. A splice can be made by means of a fishplate nailed to one or both sides of the connecting members, with a half-lap joint, a splayed lap, a scarf joint, a bolted joint or with a V splice joint (see drawings).

SPLICES AND JOINTS

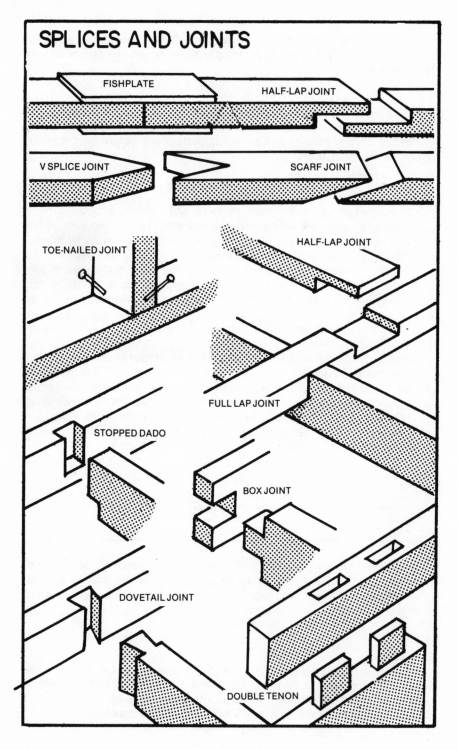

FISHPLATE

HALF-LAP JOINT

V SPLICE JOINT

SCARF JOINT

TOE-NAILED JOINT

HALF-LAP JOINT

FULL LAP JOINT

STOPPED DADO

BOX JOINT

DOVETAIL JOINT

DOUBLE TENON

SIMPLE MITER JOINT

MITER JOINT

CROSS JOINT (3)

EDGE-TO-EDGE JOINT

COPED JOINT

THREE WAY JOINTS

1

2

3

4

5

Joints

Joints are used for connections at an angle. The most common joint of all is the toe-nailed joint used for erecting wall studs. Hardware can be used to make a joint. For example, a corner brace, a T plate, and a corrugated fastener are used to make corner joints such as in wooden window screens. An overlap T joint requires only nails, screws or bolts to make.

Lap Joints

Full and half-lap joints are used for fitting cross rails flush to their meeting members. As shown in the drawings, both are simple and easy joints to make. Use a sharp backsaw and chisel to make the required cuts.

Dado Joints

The plain and stopped dado are more elegant methods of joint making. In the plain dado, the cut out area extends across the complete width of the work. In the stopped dado, the cut stops an inch or so short of the end of the work. This results in a clean-looking joint and is used quite often when appearance is a factor. The work that is to fit into the stopped dado is cut away, as shown in the drawing, to match the non-cut-out area of the dado.

Mortised Joints

A still more sophisticated joint is the mortise and tenon. It is the strongest of the T joints and is generally used in heavy framing work. The thickness of the tenon (the tongue) should never be less than one-third the thickness of the stock from which it is cut. A variation of the mortise and tenon joint is the stub tenon where the tenon goes only part way into the mortise. A double tenon is just what its name implies as shown in the drawing.

Dovetail Joints

The dovetail joint is the strongest and the most pleasing of all corner - joints. Careful marking and sharp tools are important requisites for construction. Dovetail joints fall into several categories. The most common — and most simple — is the through dovetail. A bit more complicated is the lap dovetail, often used in bookcase and drawer construction. The double lap dovetail shows the least amount of end grain but demands great care in its construction. The secret, or miter dovetail, is often used for high quality cabinet work. The knife-edge miter requires great care in its execution. See the drawings for construction details.

Box Joints

The box joint is a sort of simplified dovetail joint and is used quite often in light furniture work and drawer construction. It is of fairly easy construction and if you have access to a bench saw, the required cuts can be made in minutes.

Miter Joints

There are four methods of making a miter joint. The simplest — and the weakest — method is nailing the two meeting members together as shown in the drawing. The second method is to cut two or more slots in the top for reinforcing splines. A third method is to cut along the width of each piece to accept a single long spline as shown. The last method is to reinforce the miter joint by means of dowels. To assure accuracy in the placement of the dowels, temporarily drive a couple of brads (wire nails) into one face. Cut them off, not quite flush, and press the two pieces together so that the brads will leave their mark on the other face. Now remove the brads and drill holes for the dowels. You will get a perfect fit.

Cross-Over Joints

The simplest cross-over joint is the plain overlap. Glue, nails, or screws serve to make the joint. Another version is the cross-lap joint made by cutting a half-lap in each piece of wood. A third way of making a cross joint is by means of two or three dowels as shown in the drawing. A mitered bridle joint takes a bit more care in its construction, but it is a strong and somewhat decorative joint.

Edge-To-Edge Joints

These can be made in several ways. The easiest (therefore the most popular) method, but one that makes the weakest joint, is gluing the work together using a bar or pipe clamps as shown. Dowels make a stronger joint, but of course require accuracy in preparation. A splined joint is the strongest joint of all for edge-to-edge work. However, it does require a power saw to cut the required grooves accurately. The grooves should be slightly deeper than the spline to allow for glue expansion as glue and clamps must be used to complete the joint.

Three-Way Joints

Attaching legs in the construction of a workbench, for example, calls for an understanding of three-way joints. Illustrated in the drawings are five ways to attach legs. No. 1 is by means of a metal corner brace, a wing nut, and a hanger bolt. These corner braces are made commercially; buy them in a hardware store. Note the slots cut in the side members to accept the curved edges of the metal brace. No. 2 shows construction and assembly by means of dowels. Dowel placement should be staggered to prevent their meeting in the middle of the leg. Use two or more dowels for each leg. Nos. 3 and 4 are very similar in construction, except for the placement of the leg. No. 3 has the leg on the inside while No. 4 has the leg on the outside. No. 5 is a haunched and mitered mortise and tenon joint — it is the strongest of the leg joints. When making this joint, leave 1/4-inch or so of waste at the top of the leg and trim it off with a plane and rasp after the glue has dried.

Coped Joints

This is an important joint as it is always used in combination with a miter joint when installing ceiling and floor molding. Contrary to what many people think, there is no need to miter all four corners of molding installed at the top of the wall where it meets the ceiling. The professional will first put up two lengths of molding, at opposite sides, butting them snugly against the wall (see drawing). The other two pieces of molding are then *coped* to fit. The advantage of a coped joint is that it will hide any irregularities due to the walls not meeting at exact right angles.

If the molding is flat on the back, you can use a short piece of scrap molding as a pattern. Trace the contour as shown in the drawing on the flat side. Tape the front (to avoid splintering) and cut through the molding with a coping saw. If the molding is irregular on the back (which is usually the case with crown molding used at the ceiling), you will have to use the following technique:

First cut the molding at a 45° miter, making sure you have measured carefully. Then cut away the excess wood following the outline of the miter. As you cut away the excess wood, tilt the coping saw slightly to the long side of the molding instead of cutting straight across at a 90° angle. This way you will gain a bit of extra clearance, just in case you have left a high spot.

Making A Miter Box

In all coping and mitering operations, a miter box is essential. The miter box practically guarantees an exact 45° or 90° cut. You can buy an inexpensive miter box made of wood, or a slightly more expensive one made out of steel and adjustable for in-between angles. You can even make your own miter box — it is extremely easy to do. Knowing how to make a miter box can be a life-saver on a Sunday afternoon when all the stores are closed and you want to finish a job that requires accurate mitering. Here's how:

Nail together three pieces of wood to form a long U-shaped channel. The inside of the U can be 4 or 5 inches wide — exact size is not important, just as long as the molding can fit into it. Use a try square to mark two lines perpendicular to the two uprights as shown. Measure the *outside* width of the channel. Lay off that number of inches from each line you drew, measuring as indicated. Draw a connecting line. In effect you have laid out a square and its diagonal — and the diagonal of a square is always exactly 45°. Draw another diagonal, crossing the first one. Now use the backsaw and carefully cut across and into each diagonal line. When you reach the bottom, stop. You can now use it to cut molding at a left or right 45° angle. Complete the miter box by making a 90° cut following the outline of the perpendicular lines you first made. These 90° cuts — make two — are used to make true square cuts across molding. Surprisingly simple, wasn't it?

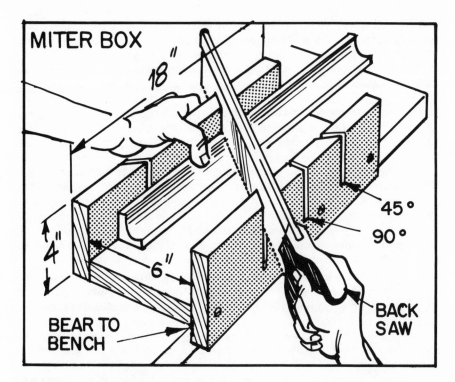

MITER BOX

18"

4"

6"

45°
90°

BACK SAW

BEAR TO BENCH

With these essential tools and materials you now have no excuse for not tackling any maintenance or repair job around the house. The next step is to find a place where you can store tools and something to work on — a workbench.

A 24-Hour Workbench

Parts for a Workbench

Two	3/4 × 24 × 60	plywood (for top)
One	1/4 × 24 × 60	tempered hardboard (for top)
Four	2 × 4 × 36	legs, cut from 2 × 4s
Four	2 × 4 × 20	crosspieces cut from 2 × 4s
Four	2 × 4 × 56	long members cut from 2 × 4s
Eight	5/16 × 4	lag bolts
Eight	5/16 × 4	roundhead bolts
Eight	1/4 X 4	carriage bolts
Sixteen	1-inch	washers
One	32-ounce	can of contact cement
One	16-ounce	container of white glue

Yes, this workbench can be built in less than a day out of readily procurable materials — 2 x 4s, hardboard, plywood, glue and some hardware. This bench is very easy to build. Sold? Then let's begin.

First cut the four legs out of the 2 x 4s; each leg is 34 inches long. Next make the upper and lower framework. Note that they are identical sets. Cut the four short lengths to the size indicated in the drawing and then cut the four longer lengths. Notch each of the four long lengths to accept the cross pieces. The notches — professionals call them "dados" — should be about 1/2-inch deep and just wide enough to fit the 2 x 4s you are using. The notch should be about 3 inches from each end as shown. Apply some white glue to the inside of the notch. Drive the two cross pieces into the notches. They should be a snug fit. Drill a clearance hole for a long 1/4-inch lag bolt (a heavy wood screw). Because you will be driving the lag bolt into the end grain of the cross piece, use fairly long lag bolts (at least 4 inches) to assure a good grip. Do the same operation to both frameworks. You will now have two oblong frames, each 60 inches long and 20 inches wide. Our finished workbench will measure 24 x 60 inches.

The next step is to fasten the four legs in place. This time we will be using 1/4 x 4-inch carriage bolts. The best way to mount the legs is to clamp them in place with C-clamps first, then drill clearance holes through the framework and through the legs for the carriage bolts. Apply some more white glue to the areas where the legs will meet the framework and pass the bolts through the clearance holes. Insert a washer and a nut and tighten securely.

After tightening, you can remove the C clamps for use on the next step, installing the second framework. Note in the drawing that the tops of the legs are flush with the upper framework. Turn the assembly upside down so that the upper framework is resting on the floor with the legs in the air. Now gently ease the second frame over the legs so that it is about 6 inches from the ends of the legs. Check with a ruler to make certain that the frame is the same distance from the legs at all four sides. Now clamp it in place, drill clearance holes as before and insert four more 1/4-inch carriage bolts, washers and nuts to finish the lower part of the workbench.

We are approaching the home stretch — the construction of the top. The top is made out of two sheets of 3/4-inch plywood, glued together and faced with a sheet of 1/4-inch tempered Masonite. Buy a single sheet of utility grade 3/4-inch 4 x 8 foot plywood. If the lumber yard will sell you a shorter length such as 4 x 5 or 4 x 6 feet, fine. Otherwise, cut the sheet in half lengthwise, then cut each piece so that it is 60 inches long. You should now have two 24 x 60-inch pieces of plywood.

Gluing the two pieces together is a comparatively easy job. Coat the top of one sheet with a layer of white glue. Squeeze the glue out of the dispenser and use a brush to distribute it evenly over the surface. Pay special attention to the corners and edges. Then carefully place the second sheet over the sheet with the glue, line up the edges, and nail the two panels together. Use annular ring nails — they hold better. No clamping is necessary as all the nail heads will be hidden by the hardboard top.

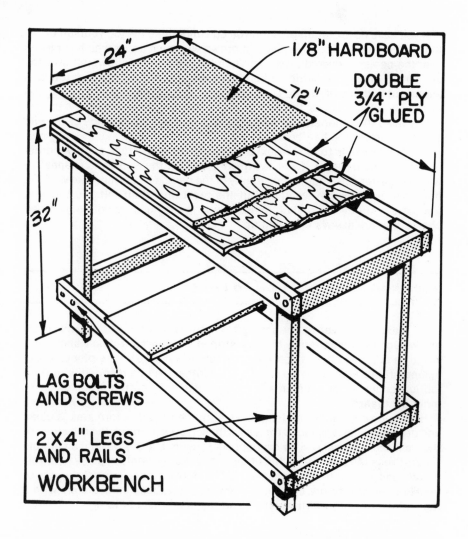

1/8" HARDBOARD

DOUBLE
3/4" PLY
/GLUED

24"

72"

32"

LAG BOLTS
AND SCREWS

2 X 4" LEGS
AND RAILS

WORKBENCH

Now cut a sheet of 1/4-inch hardboard (Masonite) to 24 × 60 inches, the same size as a glued-up top. Inasmuch as we cannot use nails to secure the hardboard to the plywood, we will have to use contact cement. Brush on the contact cement to the plywood side which has the nail-heads visible. Do the same to the hardboard (apply the contact cement to the rough surface of the hardboard). Wait around 15 minutes until the cement is no longer tacky. The next step requires an assistant — perhaps a cooperative spouse. Gently lower the hardboard over the plywood. Make sure the two are in exact alignment. Best to lower one side — a short side — and if everything is in apple-pie order, lower the rest of the panel to the plywood. This cement grabs on contact which is why later adjustment is practically impossible.

If you have no assistant on hand you can undertake the job yourself by using a "slip sheet." This is a piece of brown wrapping paper which is placed over the cement-covered plywood. Then the hardboard is lowered over the slip sheet. Adjust the hardboard until you are absolutely certain that it is in alignment with the plywood. Then raise the hardboard and pull out a section of the slip sheet. Lower the hardboard — it will grab — and you can now safely raise the other end of the hardboard, pull out the balance of the slip sheet and lower the hardboard.

That's all there is to it. The next big decision is — where to put it. A corner of the basement is fine. If you can make space for the workbench beneath a window, better yet. Another possibility is the garage — nothing like working outdoors during warm weather. But the most important thing is that you now have a sturdy workbench to assist you in the hundreds of home-repair chores that are always cropping up.

Your Work Apron and How To Fix It

An inexpensive yet important part of your working outfit should be an apron. Get the denim kind, hickory striped or blue so it won't show dirt. You'd be surprised how much wear and tear it will save your clothes. An accidental rip or tear in the apron, or your clothes can be mended with Darn fabric mender, a compound made for mending cloth, cotton, wool, rayon, or other synthetics.

Here is how to repair the tear: Make sure the ripped or torn area is clean and dry; trim away any loose threads with scissors. Apply it to both sides of the rip if the material can be overlapped. If it can't, apply Darn to a suitable patch. Press the patch — or the original material — firmly in place with your fingers and allow it to dry for at least 1/2 hour. But before using the apron, or garment, allow it to dry overnight. Remove any excess immediately with a rag moistened with warm water — and that's all there is to it.

Chapter 2

THE
BASEMENT

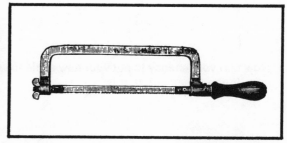

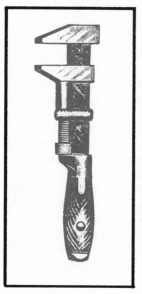

Now that you're ready to put your new skills to work, let's start at the bottom — in the basement, that is.

Door Hits Pipe

When you open the door to your basement or cellar, does it stop with a bang as it strikes an overhead pipe, that one that hangs just low enough to meet the door? A door stop will not help as the door strikes the pipes long before it ever reaches the wall. The solution is simple. You will need: a 2 × 3-inch strip of wood, E-POX-E® glue, sandpaper, hammer, and felt to cover the wood. Cut a 2 × 3-inch piece of wood (part of a furring strip is ideal) and drill a half dozen 1/4-inch holes — at random — part way through one side.

Prepare an epoxy mix using equal parts of E-POX-E resin and hardener. (Mentioned briefly on page 16 .) Good containers for mixing are plastic covers used for tennis ball cans. They have a narrow rim around the edge, and are of no earthly use when discarded — except for mixing epoxy! Swing the door open and note where it should stop before striking the pipe. At the base of the door, sand and sweep the concrete floor so that it is free of dust. Place the epoxy-coated piece of wood on the concrete floor so that the long side is parallel and in contact with the door. Tap it lightly with a hammer to make sure it is making good contact with the floor. After the epoxy has dried overnight, cement a length of felt to the side of the wood facing the door to act as a shock absorber. Try it the next morning — no more loud bang when you swing open the door to enter.

Basement Water

If there is only one problem that plagues most homeowners it is the curse of water in the basement due to seepage from the outside. This can be caused by several factors. The existing water table may be too high for the depth of the basement — in other words the builder excavated too deeply for the foundation so the basement is too low. In my community a neighbor insisted on having his home built on a grade which meant that the basement had to be lower than normal. The result? His basement gets a lot of water seepage during and after a heavy rainfall, while the people next door are higher and drier!

Another factor is grading. The land around a house should slope away from the building on all sides. If it does not, the solution is to fill in the low side of the ground with earth and grade it for a gradual slope away from the house.

Another possibility is to landscape the area around the house with lowgrowing vines and plants that will absorb moisture from the ground. For example, a pachysandra bed around the low areas will tend to absorb a good deal of ground water. In addition, the very act of cultivation loosens up the soil so that rain water tends to sink into the ground instead of collecting against the walls of the house.

Another source of unwanted water is roof water. The water that drains from the roof should be led *away* from the house by means of gutters and downspouts and not allowed to drip off the eaves and ultimately into the basement. You may already have such a system, but if the dry wells that accept rain water are not functioning then you still have a water problem.

The expense of digging new dry wells can be eliminated by having the downspouts discharge their water at least 10 feet from the house walls. This can be done by means of concrete splash blocks, a canvas pipe that uncurls (it is spring-loaded) as soon as water from the downspout enters it, and a half-round pipe, 10 feet long, connected to the lower end of the downspout to lead the water away from the walls of the house.

If you try all of these remedies and you still get some seepage, don't despair. You can lick it by checking the spots in the basement where the water enters — usually where the walls meet the floor.

To do this important job you will need a few tools — a cold chisel, a hammer, a wire brush, a vacuum cleaner, a putty knife, and epoxy cement.

First determine which areas of the basement wall are permitting the seepage. Check this during or after the next heavy rainfall. Mark the areas, then during the next dry spell use the chisel and hammer to gouge out a deep cut at the meeting line of the wall and floor (and please wear goggles). This cut should be at least an inch in depth. Next, use the wire brush to remove all loose particles. Follow this operation with the vacuum cleaner as you want to make certain that all dust and grit have been completely removed.

Next get a 10 ounce size of E-POX-E Cement & Filler if you have only a small area — less than 15 linear feet — to cover. If you are ambitious and are planning to do the entire periphery of the basement, get the gallon size. It will be less expensive in the long run.

On a clean board mix out equal amounts of resin and hardener using a separate mixing stick or spoon for each. Mix the two parts carefully according to directions until the mix is a uniform gray color. Mix only as much epoxy as you can use in 1/2 hour or so as it starts to harden as soon as it is mixed.

Apply the well-mixed compound with the putty knife. Make sure you force the compound deep into the cut. Continue the work until the entire cut-out area has been filled with the epoxy compound. Don't worry if your artistic endeavors look a little messy in spots. If you want to smooth out any rough looking areas, application of a finger moistened in water will do wonders. The epoxy will not stick to your wet finger, but make sure you wash your hands with soap and water after the job is finished.

Let the epoxy dry overnight by which time it will be as hard as a rock. Next morning you can come down to the basement and duly admire your work. We have tried this technique and can honestly say that it has cured all the leaks in the basement that occurred at the wall floor junction.

Pipe Leaks

Of course there are some leaks that come from pipes and not from ground water. What can you do? If it is a burst pipe, it's best to call in the plumber. And while he is making his unhurried way to your rapidly flooding basement, turn off the main water valve — it should be plainly labeled and all members of the family should know where it is. But, small leaks, the kind that drip due to corrosion or a faulty coupling can be repaired quite easily.

The first step is to turn off the main water supply to the house, or if that particular pipe has its own water cutoff, use it. There should be no water in the pipe you are planning to repair.

An easy way to repair this type of leak is by using the ribbon-style of epoxy. It comes in two equal lengths. (To use, tear off an equal length of each and knead them between your hands until the wad is a uniform color.) Clean the area of the water leak with a wire brush, followed by sandpaper.

Wipe the area clean and apply the E-POX-E Ribbon to the affected area. With a plastic bread wrapper or dry cleaner's bag covering your fingers, force the epoxy deep into the leak area. The plastic will allow you to remove your fingers without disturbing the seal.

Mixed E-POX-E Ribbon has a working life of about 2 hours, so there is no need to rush the job. After applying the epoxy, wash your hands with warm water and soap. Now dry your hands and admire your work.

Since it is best to let the job dry overnight, it is a good idea to tackle the repair just before going to bed so no one will be inconvenienced by lack of water. The repair will dry hard and can be painted if necessary.

But what if it's Sunday, there's no epxoy in the house and the plumber is on vacation. What then? As long as you have a C clamp among your tools or if you can borrow one from a neighbor, all is not lost. If the leak is somewhere on a straight run — not at a fitting or at a union — the C clamp and a small piece of rubber will save the day. Cut the rubber large enough to cover the leaking area — it is usually nothing more than a pinhole — and tighten the C clamp on the pipe and rubber. Use gentle pressure; you don't want to deform the pipe and enlarge the hole. Hold the clamp steady as you tighten it so it will not slip off the rounded surface of the pipe. This is a temporary repair and will serve until the plumber arrives.

A longitudinal crack in a pipe, caused by freezing, can be repaired with a special pipe clamp. The clamp consists of two half-round lengths of galvanized steel, each about 4 inches long, with a rubber lining. The rubber lining is placed around the crack in the pipe, the two halves hinged together so they will encircle the pipe and the two halves are tightened together with bolts. Such a repair, if the rest of the pipe is in good condition, actually will be a permanent repair job without having to cut out and install a new length of pipe.

Painting Basement Walls

Now that you have made your basement reasonably dry, how about sprucing it up so that you will enjoy doing all those household repair jobs in the basement work area. First tackle the walls. If they are of poured concrete, cinder blocks, or concrete blocks, they can be made quite cheerful by painting them white — but not with ordinary paint. Use white cement paint, which also has a waterproofing quality. It is available under many trade names in hardware stores and lumber yards.

The application technique for these paints is similar in most respects. The powder is mixed with water until it has the consistency of heavy cream. Hose down the walls and apply the paint with a 4-inch stiff bristle brush after the glisten of the water on the walls has gone. In other words, the walls should be damp, but not wet. Don't be too ambitious — do one short wall at a time, or half a long wall.

Now here is the important part: after the wall has dried for at least 8 hours, hose it down again. A second coat should be applied within 24 hours — and again the walls should be hosed down, just as with the first coat. Hose down the second coat after an 8-hour drying period and that's it. Remember, you have applied 2 coats of paint and 4 applications of water — all within a 24-hour period. Incidentally, only as much of the cement paint should be mixed as can be used in one painting period as it will dry within a few hours and become useless.

Don't worry if the painted walls look splotchy after you've hosed them down. This is normal and will disappear as soon as the wall is completely dry again.

A New Ceiling

Now how about covering up those exposed joists in the ceiling? Before you start nailing up ceiling tiles or plaster boards, remember that at some future time you may need access to the pipes and wiring that run under the ceiling. Most of the plumbing and a good deal of the wiring in the average house is visible in the basement.

The first solution that may come to mind is a suspended ceiling. This type of ceiling is suspended from the joists and the panels can be removed for access. The suspension will rob the basement of 4 or 5 inches of head room, but you can have your cake and eat it too if you use the following method of installing a suspended ceiling without losing any head room.

This method consists of screwing the long main runners supplied with this type of installation directly to the ceiling joists instead of suspending them from wires as is usually done. Then each tile is slid into place, one after the other. If by chance you want to get at some pipe or wire behind a particular tile, all you need to do is remove one tile at the far end and push the remaining tiles back so that the area you want is exposed. This method does away with the necessity of having to install the ceiling tiles 4 inches below the lowest pipe or drain in the basement.

In this installation only part of the basement ceiling was covered, so as to leave some of the ceiling joists available for storage. Even though the runners are 12 feet long, it is still a one person job!

The first thing we did was to paint all the main runners and the short cross trees a bright, cheerful orange to contrast with the white of the ceiling tiles. There's nothing like color to brighten up a dreary basement.

Next, we installed the first 12-foot runner by driving a nail into one joist and another nail into another joist about 10 feet from the first nail. A loop of cord was then suspended from each nail to hold the runner temporarily in place. This was the only suspension in the job.

The first runner is now in its approximate position. It is fastened to the basement ceiling joist with the 1-1/2-inch angle irons as shown in the drawing. Use an angle iron for every other joist. If the joists are uneven — as they may be — use shims (thin slips or wedges) of wood or hardboard to bring them level. Do not try to bend the runner to meet uneven joists, as the runners are quite stiff. In fact, as you install the angle irons at each end, you will quickly see where shimming is required.

After you have installed the first runner, set up the second runner, parallel to and about 4 feet from the first one; mount it temporarily with nails and cords as described before. Now use a cross tee as a measurement to fasten this second runner exactly parallel to the first runner and equal to the width of the cross tee. The runners have slots 12 inches apart and accept the "ears" of the cross tees. Insert one cross tee at each end and one in the middle to make sure the second runner is at the proper distance from the first runner. Now install this second runner with the angle irons.

You are now ready to install the first tile. These tiles, a generous 2 × 4 feet, are merely slid into place as shown in the drawing. If a little binding occurs, jiggle the tile from side to side as you keep pulling or pushing it forward. If you do come across a tight spot don't despair. Loosening one or two angle irons will give you extra leeway. Install a cross tee after each tile and then insert another tile until each row is finished. The tiles will be supported on all four sides; at each long side by means of the cross tees and at each short side by the main runners. If you have any difficulty in installing the last tile in a row, buckle it slightly and snap it in place, or since the tiles can be cut very easily, you can trim it slightly with a sharp knife and a straight edge. There is enough supporting ledge at each side to allow such trimming if necessary.

The final closure at each row is made by means of cross tees. Openings for any light fixtures are made by measuring the center point of the fixture in two directions — from one side of the main runner and from a cross tee. Cut a small opening in the tile at this point, install the tile, and finish the opening after the tile is in place. The base of the light fixture will cover the raw edges of the opening. Don't forget to turn off the electricity when working on any light fixtures that require removing and replacing.

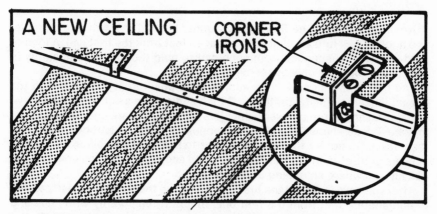

A NEW CEILING   CORNER IRONS

1.   The first step is to mount the long main runners to the ceiling joists with angle irons.

48"

2.   Space each main tee equal to the width of the cross tees. The number of main tees you will install will of course depend upon ceiling area.

3.   Install the first cross tee and then slide the first tile into place.

4. Now install another cross tee and slide the second tile into place so that it rests on the lip of the cross tee.

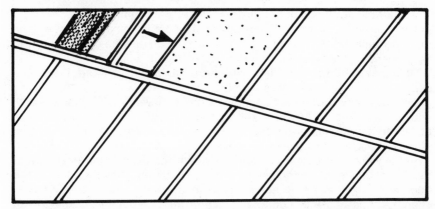

5. Continue this way until all the parallel sections you have installed have been covered by the tiles.

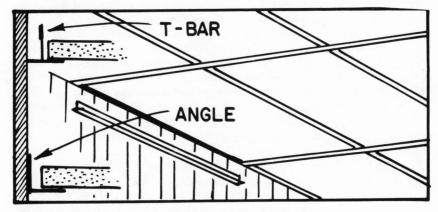

T-BAR

ANGLE

6. The final closure at each end is made with a cross tee or angle.

Painting the Basement Floor

Now that you have brightened up the walls and ceiling of your basement, it will be the floor that needs some attention. You can take care of the floor either by doing it the hard way — installing asphalt or vinyl-asphalt tiles — or by doing it the easy way and just painting the concrete floor a utilitarian gray. It is easier, faster, and much less expensive to paint the floor with a good grade of enamel rather than applying tiles, and you'll be just as pleased with the results.

If you're sold on paint, there are three types that you can use on a concrete floor that is on or below grade: latex, alkyd, or chlorinated rubber paint. Latex paint spreads easily, is low in cost and clean-up only requires warm water and soap. But it will not wear as well as the other two types and latex paint is not made in full gloss enamels, only semi-gloss.

Alkyd paint is made in full gloss enamels; cost is somewhat higher than the latex paint (about $2 more per gallon) and can only be cleaned up with paint thinner. However, it does wear better than latex paint.

Chlorinated rubber paint is a heavy duty paint for concrete floors and especially for floors that have a problem with efflorescence — that chalky growth that many concrete floors below ground level develop. It wears well and is not affected by the alkali in the concrete. Some preparation is necessary before using this paint. If it is a new concrete floor it should be etched with a mixture of one part of hydrochloric acid to three parts of water. Pour the water into a glass container and then add the acid (never add water to acid). It is best to wear gloves and goggles. Scrub a small section of the floor, about 10 feet by 10 feet with this mixture. Use a stiff bristle brush. Then flush the area with plenty of water until all traces of the acid have been eliminated. Treat the entire floor this way.

Old floors do not require the acid-water treatment, but those areas of the floor which show efflorescence should be given this preparation.

Wait until the floor is completely dry before starting to paint. Vacuum a small section of the floor. Stir the paint so that it is a uniform color and apply the paint with a 4-inch brush, covering a single vacuumed area at a time. A gallon of paint will cover about 250 square feet. A second coat, which is recommended, will cover about 300 square feet. Allow the paint to dry for at least three or four days before you start moving equipment back in place.

Painting with Alkyd paint is about the same as using the chlorinated rubber paint except the acid etching treatment can be eliminated, especially if it is an old floor.

Regardless of which paint you use, there are a few precautions to observe. Even though chlorinated rubber paint and alkyd paint can be thinned with the same thinner, *the paints are not compatible.* If you mix these two paints together, they will curdle — so don't do it. Also, a chlorinated rubber paint may lift old alkyd or latex paint. So before using chlorinated rubber paint, try it on a small section of the floor and examine it the next day. If no lifting has occured, it is safe to go ahead. And of course never mix latex paint with an alkyd paint.

As a finishing touch, paint the floor up the wall area to a height of about 4 inches; it makes an effective baseboard.

Water Hammer

Are you treated to a concert of bangs, clatters and knocks every time you turn off a water faucet? This is due to a phenomenon known as water hammer. Water cannot be compressed, so when it is brought to a sudden stop by turning off the faucet, it has nowhere to go, but its momentum keeps it going. This makes a banging, knocking noise as it comes to rest. Turning the faucet off slowly may help, but this is impossible with toilet flushometers and washing machines that turn off the water automatically.

The answer is the installation of a water hammer arrestor. They are made in various styles, but basically consist of a cylinder or globe that contains air. It is the air that absorbs the force of the water. They should be installed in a pipe as close as possible to the noisy fixture. If this is impossible, have the installation made at some point in the basement where the pipes serving the particular faucet can be worked on.

But before going to such an expense try the following two remedies: first, make sure all the water pipes in the house are secured to joists, walls, or to any other convenient support by means of pipe straps. A pipe strap every 48 inches is a good rule to follow. Use copper straps if the pipes are copper or brass. But the strap should be secured around the pipe in such a way that expansion and contraction of the pipe is permitted. One way to do this is to cement a half-circle of felt to the inside of the strap. The felt has just enough "give" to allow the pipe to move during its expansion and contraction cycle (this is especially important with hot water pipes) and yet will prevent the pipe from clattering against the wall.

The second possible remedy is to allow air to get into the piping system. This can be done after the family has gone to bed. Open up the topmost faucet in the house — usually a shower on an upper floor — and open up the lowest faucet — usually the washtub in the basement. Then turn off the main water supply valve. The water in the lines will then drain out through the lowest faucet and air will enter the system.

The next morning, close both valves and turn on the main water supply valve. The air in the pipes will now act as a cushion for the water. This will only work for a couple of months or so, until the air has been absorbed by the water (you will know when this has occurred because that horrible banging will start again) but it's well worth trying.

Chapter 3

BATHROOM REPAIRS

When it comes to building a house, the bathroom and the kitchen are the two most expensive rooms in it. So, it pays to keep a critical eye on these two rooms and make immediate repairs to their appliances.

Broken Soap Dish

A frequent problem in the bathroom is a chipped or loose soap dish or toothbrush holder. Chipping is especially prevalent, usually because of an overloaded medicine cabinet. When the door of the cabinet is open, out falls a jar, or can, chipping the soap dish on its way to the sink. Quite often the sink is chipped as well.

Aside from trying not to overload the cabinet, one method of preventing such accidents is to cut a piece of vinyl molding (sold at auto supply stores), the kind with a U-shaped channel, to the exact length of the shelf and force it over the edge of the glass, creating a lip at the edge of the shelf. By doing this to each shelf in the cabinet you will help to prevent those all-too-numerous jars from having a free fall.

If the descending jar of cold cream has knocked off a corner of the soap dish and you have the missing part in one piece, the repair can be quite easy. Make sure the raw edges of the parts to be matched are perfectly clean and dry. if you make the repair as soon as the mishap has occurred, there's no problem. But if you have procrastinated (like most of us) clean both surfaces with an old toothbrush dipped in rubbing alcohol. After giving both pieces a good scrub, apply a single drop of Super Glue® -3 to about 1 square inch of the broken off piece. *Do not apply the glue to the part remaining in the wall.* Only one surface need be treated and it is easier to apply the glue to the piece in your hand. Now immediately fit the piece in your hand to the fixture part. Don't wait. Never mind if the phone rings; keep pressing the parts together for 30 seconds or so. This is plenty of time for the glue to do its job.

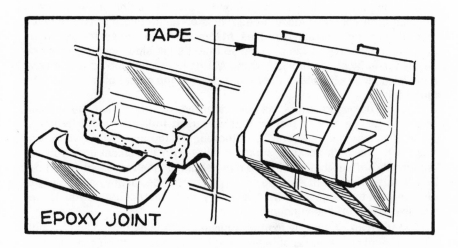

Large Breaks

How about mending a large broken off piece? It would be best to support the piece during the drying and curing of the glue.

Clean the areas to be joined. Then mix up the epoxy compound using an equal quantity of resin and hardener — careful: do not contaminate one can with the contents of the other. Stir thoroughly. (The mix will be a uniform gray if you are using the black and white epoxy mixes or a clean white if you are using the "white" kind. The white type is recommended for porcelain repairs.)

Now apply a thin layer of epoxy to each surface, and pressing them firmly together, apply masking tape to the wall, over the fixture, and then below on the wall surface. This should hold the mended parts firmly together until the epoxy has cured. Strip away the tape the next morning. Any excess epoxy can be removed by careful scraping with a sharp knife or a single-edge razor blade. A repair made with epoxy is impervious to water, alcohol, and most solvents.

Installing A New Soap Dish

The damage to the soap dish, toothbrush holder, or toilet paper dispenser may be so complete that a new fixture is required. First, you will have to remove the old one. This may take more time than installing a new one — but it can be done. The toughest part of the job will be removing the broken fixture from its recess.

Get a sharp awl from your tool kit and score the outline of the fixture in the wall until you have made a deep incision all around the fixture, being careful not to chip the adjacent tiles. At this point use a chisel to deepen the cut. Place the chisel in the opening so that the flat side faces the tiles and beveled side faces the broken fixture. A little judicious tapping with a hammer should serve to loosen the fixture, even to the extent of breaking off a piece or two.

After the damaged fixture has been removed, you must clean the opening of all mortar, cement or plaster that was used to keep the old fixture in place. If this step is not done quite thoroughly, the new fixture will not fit flush with the wall, so keep scraping away with the chisel until you are reasonably certain that all of the old material has been removed. Insert the new fixture for a trial fit — if the new fixture protrudes at any area, continue cleaning out the recess. If it fits too deeply, don't let that bother you. Better too deep than not deep enough.

Coat the back of the new fixture — make sure it is perfectly clean — with a thin layer of epoxy and apply a few dabs of the epoxy to the recess to be on the safe side. Press the new fixture into place. If it sets too deeply in the recess, pull it out slightly until it is flush with the wall surface. Use tape to support the fixture until the epoxy has cured overnight. Curing can be hastened by applying heat; just direct an infra-red heat lamp, sunlamp, or photoflood lamp to the repair for 10 minutes or so. Keep the lamp at least 2 feet away from the job.

Any epoxy that has oozed out can be removed with a damp cloth provided it is done within 1/2-hour. Also, a moistened finger can be used to smooth out any irregularities in the epoxy joint (epoxy will not stick to a wet surface). And, if you have used the "gray" epoxy because you did not have any "white" on hand, the seam can be whitened to match existing tiled areas by rubbing some plaster-of-paris into the seam. Do this before the epoxy has had a chance to set. Wipe off excess plaster with a damp cloth.

Damaged Shower Handles

Broken off shower handles — especially the ceramic kind — are expensive, hard to match, but easy to repair with epoxy or Super Glue-3. All you need to do is apply a drop of this glue to the broken off part (make sure it is perfectly clean) — just a single drop and place it in immediate contact with the rest of the handle — and that's it. The repair is fast and convenient.

Repairing Chips In Porcelain

How about a chipped area on the bathroom sink? Such a chip can be made as good as new by using Porcelain Repair, an acrylic that is non-yellowing and withstands heat up to 350°.

First make sure that the area to be repaired is clean, absolutely free of oil, rust, or dirt. A toothbrush dipped in rubbing alcohol will do a good cleaning job. If the appliance to be repaired is white, then apply the Porcelain Repair just as it comes out of the tube. But, if the repair is to be on a colored porcelain, it can be colored with artist's colors. Only a very small amount of coloring will be necessary as most colored bathroom fixtures are in pastel shades. Squeeze a little of the medium out of the tube and add a drop of the coloring. Mix with a matchstick or a paper clip until the desired color has been achieved. Keep the mix on the light side rather than the dark side. This is really a matter of trial and error. When you have the right color, apply the mixture to the chip or gouge. It will dry to the touch in about 10 minutes. Any excess can be removed with nail polish remover or with lacquer thinner. *Caution:* No more than 10% by volume of artist's color should be mixed with the Porcelain Repair. Too much will affect its "sticking" qualities.

Ceramic Floor Tile Repairs

Broken, missing, or chipped ceramic tiles in the bathroom floor should be replaced as soon as possible to prevent water from seeping into the floor boards below the tiles.

The first step is, of course, to remove the offending tiles. This can be done by light chipping with a chisel and hammer. Wear goggles, as ceramic splinters are just as sharp as glass. After the tiles have been removed, clean out the old cement in the recess with a screwdriver or chisel. Clean thoroughly and finish this part of the job by vacuuming.

If you do not have any extra tiles on hand, you are left with two choices. Either visit a tile store — with a sample tile in hand — and buy enough tiles to make the repair. (Ceramic tiles are sold only in sheet form. The tiles are cemented to heavy paper and in the original installation the sheet of tiles is placed into a bed of cement with the paper facing up. After a day or so, the paper is moistened and peeled off.) Ceramic tile stores are listed in the classified telephone directory.

Or, if only one or two tiles need replacing, try the following method: Make up an epoxy mix, colored with artist's oil colors or even paint to match the existing tiles. Mix up the epoxy according to directions and stir in enough color to match the existing tiles. (Remember, the amount of color mixed in should not be more than 10% by volume,) then ladle the mix into the space, smooth it out with a wet spatula so that it is even with the rest of the floor, and let it dry overnight.

Tiles that are cracked and still in place can be repaired by lifting out the loose parts of the tile, coating the cleaned edges and bottom with the epoxy mix and replacing them. Make sure the replaced tiles are even with the rest of the floor by placing a board over the repaired area and pressing down so that all the tiles are in firm contact with the bottom of the board.

Tile and Fixture Care

Cam-Kleen® ceramic tile and grout cleaner, in an aerosol can, is especially made for cleaning bathroom tiles, the grout between the tiles, and the fixtures in the bathroom. It is easy to use, contains no abrasives, and there's no need to scrub away. Leave it on for a few minutes, wipe away the foam with a rag, and follow with another rag, rinsed in clean water.

To clean the grout between the tiles, use a brush to force the foam between the tiles. An old toothbrush is fine for this operation. Use the heavy duty liquid version for really tough jobs.

To *keep* your bathroom clean, use Cam-Kote® Tile Polish and sealer. Much quicker and easier than waxing, it effectively prevents grime from adhering to the walls and fixtures, and will keep the bathroom worthy of a VIP visit.

Sealing Leaks Around The Bathtub

One perennial chore in the bathroom is trying to keep a good seal between the rim of the bathtub and the surrounding wall. "Impossible," the average homeowner will swear. No matter how many times he or she seals this area around the tub — usually with plaster-of-paris — the next week or so, the inevitable crack appears. Why? When you fill the tub with water and gingerly stip into it, a weight of about 400 pounds pushes the tub down to the floor and away from its seal. And when you leave the tub and drain the water, the tub will try to regain its original position — joists under the tub area are elastic — and so the seal is broken because of the constant flexing and repositioning of the tub as it is filled, used, and drained.

The best cure for this headache is a flexible compound for sealing the joint — such as a tub and tile caulk. The chief virtue of this product — it has others as well — is its extreme flexibility. Furthermore, it will always stay white and is mildew-resistant.

Clean the area around the tub. Scrape out all the old sealing compound with a putty knife and a screwdriver, and use a vacuum cleaner to remove all dust and grit. Wipe the area with a damp cloth, followed with a dry cloth. Squeeze out the sealer from the tube and force it as deeply as you can into the crack. Go all around the periphery of the tub paying special attention to corner areas. Any slight irregularities in application can be smoothed with a moistened finger tip. Remove any excess with a moistened rag.

If the tub and wall are colored, the caulk can be painted after it has dried for a few days. Because of its silicone content, it will actually repel water rather than absorbing it as plaster-of-paris will do.

Installing Fixtures

How about installing a bathroom fixture where none existed? A hook for hanging a towel or robe for example. You don't want to take the chance of cracking the ceramic tile by drilling a hole in it and you simply cannot screw or nail it to the tiles. But you can attach a hanger capable of heavy-duty work to ceramic tile. It's really not hard to do with a fixture adhesive.

Clean the area where you want the hanger to be installed and clean the back of the hanger as well. Squeeze out enough of the material to cover the back of the hanger and immediately press it to the chosen area. It will hold, but wait a few hours before using the hook.

If you are in a real hurry to use the hook, pull the bonded item away from the wall, wait 5 minutes, and then press it back into place. But if you are planning to use the adhesive to hang a heavy object, it is best to support the item with adhesive tape or even a broomstick propped under the piece until it dries.

Removing Stains

If you allow a faucet to drip too long before repairing it, you will be assured of a stain in the sink, toilet bowl, or bathtub. Copper or brass pipes will reward you with a green stain while galvanized steel pipes show a brown stain. How can you remove these stains (after fixing the leaking faucet, of course)?

A modern solution to the old stain problem is to use Tub 'n Sink Jelly™ to remove stubborn stains from porcelain fixtures by means of a chemical reaction instead of by abrasives and muscle power. It will also remove stains from plastic shower stalls and bathtubs.

Brush or wipe it on the spot liberally. Then let it go to work for 5 to 10 minutes and rinse with water. If the stain reappears, repeat the application. Because of the strength of its chemical content, use rubber or plastic gloves when working with it, and do not leave it on the surface for more than 10 minutes. Also, *do not use* it on *cracked* or *abraded porcelain surfaces*. When using it on a toilet bowl, remove the water from the bowl. This product is also recommended for dissolving lime and hard water discoloration from fiberglass and acrylic surfaces.

A Shaver Outlet

What with the prevalence of electric razors, there is no reason why the bathroom should not have an extra outlet for the razor. If your bathroom lacks an outlet and you have a wall-mounted light fixture — usually over the medicine cabinet — it is an easy matter to install an outlet. Simply remove the existing wall fixture (which is normally controlled by the wall switch) and replace it with a light fixture that also has a convenience outlet. The only drawback with this arrangement is that the outlet is only "live" when the light is on. But, that is a minor drawback as you always want the light on when shaving.

Suppose the bathroom has a ceiling light controlled by a wall switch — what then? You will have to install a new outlet somewhere on the wall next to the mirror on the medicine cabinet. Not as hard a procedure as you may think.

You will need a length of BX cable (length depends upon how far away the nearest wall outlet is located). In addition, you need an outlet box, a duplex receptacle, and a cover plate. Locate the nearest and most accessible wall outlet. If you are in luck it will be in the next room on the other side of the wall.

Make certain that the outlet on the opposite side of the wall is not controlled by a wall switch. Our neighbor made an embarassing mistake when he wired the new outlet to an existing outlet in the living room, and then realized the living room had the arrangement common in many homes — the wall switch controls the lamps plugged into the wall outlet. If the bathroom is under the attic, look up there for a junction box you can splice into.

Next, determine just where you want to install the outlet on the wall. The outlet should be shoulder height and, if possible, above the tiled area of the bathroom, so that you won't have to cut an opening in the glazed tile. Cut an opening 1/8-inch larger all around than the dimension of the outlet box. Cutting this hole will give you an idea of where the studs are located in the wall and how best to snake the BX cable from the existing outlet or junction box to the new outlet.

Now visit the fuse box or circuit breaker box, and turn off the current that supplies electricity to the junction box or outlet from which you will be running the BX cable. Do not worry about overloading the circuit; electric razors draw very little current — less than a 10 watt bulb.

If you choose to wire your new outlet into a junction box, the task is somewhat easier than with an outlet box. First remove the coverplate. The junction box will contain a rat's nest of wires, some black and some white. Remove enough tape from the wires to expose one black wire and one white wire. (Some junction boxes may contain a red wire as well; ignore it and stick to the black wire. The red wire has the same electrical value as a black wire — hot!) Pull out or remove enough of the BX cable to expose about 4 inches of the two wires inside the cable. Punch out one of the knockout plugs in the junction box and insert a locknut in the hole. Tighten this locknut securely with pliers. Next insert an insulating collar around the wires where they emerge from the cable (see drawing) and pass the wires and cable through the locknut. Tighten the set screw on the locknut to hold the cable securely.

Now scrape off 2 inches of insulation from each wire. The wires should be clean, bright, and free of any shreds of insulation; the same applies to the two wires in the junction box you have previously cleaned. Connect the black wire to the cleaned black wire and the white wire to the cleaned white wire. Remember: *It is always white to white and black to black.*

The next step is to "snake" the cable to the cutout area in the bathroom. The drawings will give you a good idea of how this can be done. A little ingenuity and patience will always be required. Now that you have passed the cable through the bathroom wall opening, punch out one of the plugs in the box and insert a locknut, just as you did in the junction box. Strip the wires, insert an insulating collar, pass the cable through the locknut, and tighten the setscrew.

The next step is to fasten the outlet box securely to the wall. There are a couple of ways this can be done. If the wall opening is next to a wall stud, screw the box to the stud. (You will have to use an offset screwdriver for this job.) Or, you can use a mounting flange especially designed for mounting a box in what is called "old work." Visit your hardware store for this item.

"Snaking" the cable to outlet.

Remove cover plate and unscrew old switch's mounting screws.

Attach new switch to same wires and screw into box.

BORING TOOL

WIRE WITH HOOK ENDS

After the box has been securely mounted in the wall a little ingenuity may be required. Scrape off 1/2-inch of insulation from each wire. Make a loop at each end in a clockwise direction and attach the wires to the receptacle. *Note:* The screws on one side of the receptacle are brass and on the other side they are nickel-plated. *Connect the black wire to the brass screw and the white wire to the nickel-plated screw.* The extra screws are for continuing the wiring process to another outlet — if you are that ambitious.

Now gently ease the wired receptacle into the box and use the two screws that came with the receptacle to secure it to the outlet box. Attach the cover plate. Go to the fuse box and turn on the current. Plug your razor into the outlet and you should be rewarded with a pleasant hum indicating a job well done.

A connection from an existing outlet will be a bit more difficult because of cramped working conditions. Remove the receptacle from the box and then remove the wires; this will give you added work space. Next, remove the metal outlet box from the wall. This is necessary in order to mount the locknut and to pass the cable through the locknut. Thereafter the process is the same as when working with a junction box.

Passing cable from one part of the house to another is not as difficult as it may appear — after all, electricians do it all the time. Sometimes a cable can be passed where needed via the basement or as we indicated before, through the attic.

Toilet Tank Adjustments And Repairs

There is nothing quite so annoying as a toilet tank that keeps on flushing, or running. The first thing to do is to check the float, that big ball connected by a wire or rod to the water supply. As the water rises, during the filling stage, the float keeps moving up and, when the tank is full should turn off the valve feeding water into the tank.

If the water keeps running, then the float is not turning off the valve. This can be corrected by bending the rod that supports the float *downwards* so the float will turn off the water sooner, before it reaches the overflow pipe.

The water may still keep running if the tank ball stopper is not seating properly. Check to make sure it is moving smoothly up and down in its guide. If necessary, loosen the guide and adjust it so the tank ball stopper moves freely.

If the water still keeps running, check the fit of the tank ball stopper on its seat. It may be riding too high. If so, lower it by moving its rod into the next *lower* hole in the horizontal arm (this is the arm that is connected to the lever on the outside of the toilet tank). Some tanks have chains holding the tank ball stopper, in this case, just lengthen the chain.

Water still running? Check the bottom of the ball stopper. It is made of soft rubber and in time will wear away.

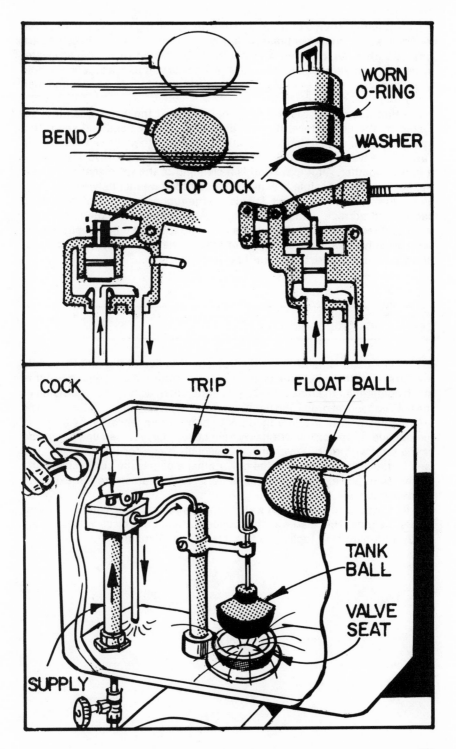

BEND

WORN O-RING

WASHER

STOP COCK

COCK

TRIP

FLOAT BALL

TANK BALL

VALVE SEAT

SUPPLY

One potential source of trouble to look for is the big ball float itself. Even though made of copper or brass, it may have sprung a leak and become partly filled with water. Unscrew the float from its arm and shake it. If any water is inside, drain the water, locate the hole, and clean the area around the hole with steel wool. Mend the hole with epoxy, let it dry for a few hours and then screw the float back on its arm.

Another trouble spot is the valve that shuts off the water when it is actuated by the float. Move the float all the way up by hand and see if this stops the water from entering the tank. If it doesn't, then the valve is at fault. Turn off the water supply to the tank and disassemble the valve, noting how it is put together. All it may need is a cleaning of the valve seat and a new washer. Another possible leak may be a corroded washer between the tank drain pipe and the toilet bowl. This is a large rubber washer which tends to harden and corrode with age. The only remedy is to take the connection apart and replace the washer with a new one. Squirt some penetrating oil such as Solvo-Rust® super penetrant around the locknut as it is no doubt firmly rusted in place, before starting this job.

Toilet Tank Condensation

This is a common and annoying problem. It is due to the fact that while the outside of the toilet tank is at room temperature, the incoming water is much colder than the tank wall. Condensation then occurs on the outside of the tank collects in drops and finally lands on the floor.

One remedy is to insulate the tank to prevent condensation by covering the outside of the tank with a heavy "slipcover." Or, you can line the *inside* of the tank with rigid polyurethane especially made for this purpose. The tank is drained and dried and the polyurethane panels are cut to shape and cemented in place. If a careful job is done, and no areas are left exposed, condensation will be stopped.

A third way is to tap the hot water supply so a mix of hot and cold water enters the tank. This also will stop condensation, but unless you are really handy with plumbing tools, this is a job for the plumber.

Chapter 4

KITCHEN CHORES

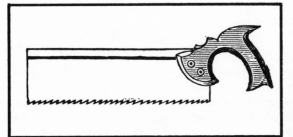

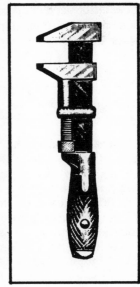

The kitchen is probably the busiest room in the house, as well as being the most expensive to "furnish" and maintain. The standard appliances — sink, range, dishwasher — and the electrical and plumbing work needed for them can be costly, and it is this room that bears the most traffic and abuse. Between the uproar of daily meal cooking and clean-up, and the numerous family projects undertaken in the kitchen, even brand-new applicance, countertops and floors can soon look battered and old. A typical kitchen has a number of different kinds of surfaces — porcelain, enamel, Formica, vinyl — and they all require different treatments to keep them looking new.

Mending Dishes and Glassware

Breakage can run high in the kitchen, and a lot is discarded, but many broken items made of china, glass and porcelain can be rescued and made to look almost as good as new. All you need is the right adhesive, something to hold parts together, some touchup paint and a little patience.

E-POX-E glue is recommended for repairing items where chips or small pieces are missing. It can even be used to build up and model missing pieces. The joint is very strong, can withstand repeated dishwashing, and is not as brittle as that formed with a cyanoacrylate. Super Glue-3 will do an excellent job when pieces fit perfectly snug, such as a broken handle on a vase.

Begin by gathering all the broken pieces together. Wash them with detergent and water, and allow them to dry thoroughly. Wipe the edges with a cloth dipped into a solvent such as lighter fluid or denatured alcohol. Avoid touching these edges with your fingers because skin oil can interfere with a good bond.

After you have cleaned each piece, put them together without using glue to decide how they belong, and plan a method of holding them while they dry. It is usually best to start with the largest pieces. When there are three or more parts, the job will probably be done in stages to allow the first joints to set before continuing with the rest.

Rubber bands, masking or cellophane tape, or strips of cloth may be used to hold the parts in position while the adhesive hardens. Plastic putty or modeling clay makes a good support when molded into the shape and size you need or to hold upright pieces stuck into it.

Mix the epoxy when you are ready to assemble the parts with glue. Apply to both edges, and after the pieces are assembled, wipe all excess away. If this is difficult, let the adhesive dry until it is slightly stiff, and use a razor to shave off the excess material.

If you are using Super Glue, you need only apply it to one surface. One drop per square inch is sufficient. Spread out the drop and immediately squeeze the parts together. Keep the pressure on for 10 seconds or until the bond sets. It will be completely hardened in a few more minutes. To remove excess glue, pour nail polish remover on a cloth and lay the cloth on glue to be removed. After approximately one minute, glue will soften and be easy to wipe up.

If the supporting tapes or other clamping devices are removed before the adhesive is completely hardened, the problem of stocking at the glue line is lessened, and excess material can be carefully shaved off. However, if the glue line is visible, it can be covered with model enamel or lacquers or paints made especially for decorating china and glass. They are found in most hobby shops and come in many different colors which are easily blended to match your shade. Use a fine pointed water color brush and paint over the objectionable line until it disappears. Allow to dry, and it's ready to use.

Touching Up Cuts and Scratches

For enamel or porcelain surfaces that are not subject to high temperatures, a high-grade glaze such as appliance touch-up paint will take care of any cuts or scratches. To use, make sure the area to be treated has been thoroughly cleaned and is perfectly dry. Apply the compound with a small brush. It will dry in 10 minutes, but keep away from the touched-up area until the next day. Excess material can be cleaned up with lacquer thinner or nail polish remover. Appliance touch-up paints are available in most popular colors to match most of those used by appliance manufacturers today. Remember, this product can't be used on "hot" surfaces such as ranges or broilers.

For appliances that are subject to high heat (such as the kitchen range, the broiler and the toaster) you will need porcelain repair. This glaze withstands temperatures up to 350°, does not yellow and can be used on any metal or porcelain surface.

First, clean the chipped or scratched area, so that it is free of dirt, and especially kitchen grease. Apply the compound with a small brush or a bit of cloth. Be careful not to get it on any unwanted surfaces; but if the inevitable happens, wipe it off with a rag moistened with nail polish remover.

Caution: Do not apply while an appliance is still hot. Wait until it is at room temperature. Porcelain repair will touch-dry in 10 minutes; maximum hardness is achieved overnight. If a second coat is needed, allow the first coat to dry overnight before the second application. This product can also be used for mending small chips in dinnerware as it is dishwasher safe after drying.

Refinishing Appliances

If your refrigerator, dishwasher, or any other appliance in the kitchen is very badly scratched — and possibly yellowed by its proximity to the kitchen range, or if you just want a new color in the kitchen, then an overall refinishing may be in order. This can be done easily with E-Pox-E Enamel, an aerosol-packed enamel which dries to a super-hard porcelain-like finish.

Since preparation and clean-up is 90% of any paint job, begin by moving the appliance to the middle of the kitchen. If you can't, tape newspaper to nearby walls and other furniture to catch any over-spray.

The next step is to make certain that the appliance, or that part of it that you want to refinish, is carefully cleaned. No dirt, grease, soap, or any other extraneous material should be on the surface. Sand the area with fine sandpaper or rub it down well with fine steel wool. Now wipe the surface with a cloth slightly dampened with paint thinner.

Shake the can for a few minutes to make certain the contents are thoroughly mixed (there is a steel ball inside the can to expedite this chore), and make a trial spray on some newspaper to make certain the paint comes out in an even mist and isn't sputtering.

If all is well, start to spray, holding the can about 12 inches from the surface. Start at the top, and at all times keep the can an even distance from the work. *Do not spray by twisting your wrist.* If you do, you will be spraying in an arc and the enamel will be deposited unevenly. Move your arm from side to side.

It is best to apply a second coat, especially if the original coat was another color, or was in bad condition. Wait about 10 minutes before applying this second coat, but do not wait longer than 2 hours. Within this time period, the second coat will "meld" into the first coat making for a smooth, even surface. After the work is finished, clean the nozzle by turning the can upside down and spray for a few seconds until only the propellant — the gas — emerges from the nozzle. This product can be used on wood, metal, porcelain — in fact on most surfaces, except plastics.

Loose Floor Tiles

This common occurrence is usually the result of faulty installation or traffic before the cement used for laying the tiles had a chance to dry. If the tiles are asphalt or vinyl-asphalt, do not attempt to pry them up as they will be sure to crack. Instead, apply moderate heat with a flatiron until that part of the loose tile — and a bit beyond — is uncomfortably warm to the touch. Then bend it up (*slowly,* please, otherwise the tile may crack). Vinyl tiles are flexible, asphalt tiles are not.

Prop up the tile with a block of wood, and scrape off as much as you can of the old cement from the bottom of the tile and from the floor. Pay special attention to the corner areas. If the going is tough, try a solvent to loosen the cement. First try warm water, as the original tiles may have been installed with a water-solvent paste. If this has no effect, try paint thinner. But be careful not to lift the adjoining tiles or to get any of the thinner — or water — under them.

When you have removed as much of the old cement as you can, wipe the bottom of the tile and the floor area with a rag. Make sure there are no crumbs of old cement left on the floor area, which if left will show up as bumps on the tile surface. Now lower the tile for a "dry" fit. It should fit in place without any projections. If it doesn't, remove more of the old cement. Now you are ready for the actual cementing. Using a fixture adhesive, apply it to the floor area *only.* This need be applied to one surface only. Use a narrow putty knife, if necessary, to spread the adhesive around.

Now lower the tile in place, pound it down with your fist and then place a smooth board over the tile and weight the board with a couple of bricks. Remove the weight and the board the next day. You may see a slight ridge along one edge, but don't let it bother you. Sand down that area carefully until it is flush with the adjacent tiles. Modern-day tiles have their color running all the way through to the back.

Replacing Floor Tiles

Sometimes the damage on a floor tile may be so extensive that complete replacement of the tile is the only remedy. Even if you have spare tiles on hand, or can buy duplicates, bear in mind that they will not match the old tiles exactly, because old tiles have by now been subject to considerable wear. But, since kitchen floors are so heavily-traveled, it won't be long before the new tiles look just like the old ones.

The obvious first step is to remove the old tiles. Start by scoring a deep line all around the boundary of the tile that needs removal. Go over the scored line several times until you are sure the knife has penetrated to the floor. If the tiles are asphalt or asphalt-vinyl, chip an opening in the center and work toward each edge to remove the tile. After the initial break has been made, use a putty knife or a broad chisel to remove the rest of the tile. Vinyl tiles can be removed by lifting one corner and peeling it away from the floor.

When all the tiles to be replaced have been removed, scrape all the old cement from the floor. Try warm water first as the original adhesive may have been water-based. A broad chisel and a hammer will do wonders in removing old, encrusted cement. Remove as much as you can then use a stiff brush and warm water to remove any residue still on the floor.

If the water has no effect on the cement, try paint thinner. (Make sure you have good ventilation in the room.) Pay particular attention to corners; avoid lifting adjacent tiles. Try the new tiles for fit. Just to make certain that they will fit without any urging, sand down the bottom four edges of each tile — a sort of beveling operation. This will assure a good installation, especially if there is the slightest bit of adhesive still left along the edge.

Wipe the surface and apply a coat of fixture adhesive to the cleaned floor area. Excess adhesive can be removed with a moistened rag. Professional tile installers (the conscientious kind) always use a heavy roller to assure a good contact between tile, cement, and the floor. You can get equally good results — even better — if you place a board and a heavy weight over the newly tiled area. Caution: Let the family know where the board is so they won't trip over it in the dark and ruin your work!

Tiles (and carpeting) show the greatest wear at all entrances in the house, so it's always a good idea to hold on to extra tiles and carpet remnants.

Repairing Countertops

Countertops, whether made of vinyl, Formica, or Micarta, are subject to considerable wear in the kitchen. Quite often the area immediately to the right and left of the sink will start to wear out long before the rest of the countertop shows any wear. This is because pots, pans, and dishes are always placed there during the food preparation or washing. A more urgent reason for repairing a countertop is a burn caused by removing a pan from the kitchen range and inadvertantly placing it on the counter next to the range.

Replacing the entire countertop is expensive, expecially if the sink is involved but without too much difficulty you can install a patch of new material without having to call in a professional. With a knife and a steel straightedge to guide it, cut out a square or rectangle of the countertop that encompasses the damaged area. Tape the straightedge to the countertop so it will not slip.

Repeat the cuts until you are sure that you have gone down to the plywood base of the countertop. Now lift off the damaged piece, being careful not to disturb the adjacent area. Clean out all the old cement with a solvent such as lacquer thinner (use adequate ventilation and avoid smoking or any open flame while doing this job). Make sure all of the cement has been removed from the area. To get a new piece of Formica, go to a dealer specializing in countertop work with the cut out piece and see if you can buy a small piece matching what you have in hand. If one store doesn't have your pattern in stock, try another. Visit a few if necessary, and check the Classified section of your telephone book. But, if you have absolutely no luck matching pieces, then get a piece that will either make a pleasant contrast to the existing countertop or will harmonize with it. In fact, you may want to make a patch on either side of the sink for balance.

Now that you now have a generous piece of the replacement on hand, the next step is to cut it to the exact size of the opening. If you have access to a power saw use a blade with fine teeth — band saw, jig saw, or bench saw. If you're cutting by hand, use a backsaw. Cut from the front of the Formica so that chips, if any, will be on the back. Formica can also be scored and snapped. But, first make several deep cuts, nearly to the back, before trying to snap the material. It would be better to practice this technique on some scrap material.

When cutting the Formica, cut it slightly oversize rather than undersize. The final fitting can be done by sanding. Next, get a can of contact cement. Stir the contents and apply a coat of cement to the patch and to the opening. Allow to dry for at least 10 minutes or until the surfaces are no longer tacky to the touch. Carefully lower one edge of the patch into place, making sure that the fit is exact. Then lower the rest of the patch into place. Immediately apply pressure, by means of a roller (a darkroom print roller will do) or by rubbing and pounding with a rag around your hand. Any excess cement can be removed with lacquer thinner or nail polish remover.

Repairing a Vinyl Countertop

You can use a somewhat different technique to repair a countertop made of vinyl if you can get an exact replacement for the repair. If you have a spare piece on hand or can buy some, tape the piece over the burned or damaged area. Make sure it is big enough to extend an inch or so beyond the damaged area. Then cut through both the replacement piece on top and the damaged piece on bottom. Keep cutting away until you are certain that the knife cut has penetrated to the wood underneath. This is known as making a Dutch cut and is used by professional paperhangers to make clean, true-fitting joints. You can check the progress of your work by lifting one corner to see if the knife cuts have penetrated to the bottom. One great advantage of this type of cut is that the cut can be irregular to follow the outlines of the damaged area, or any other shape the artist in you dictates.

After the cut has been made, lift off the top and bottom pieces. The top piece should now have the exact shape of the damaged piece that was removed and of course the same shape as the exposed opening. This operation is best done with a vinyl countertop which is softer than Formica.

Now clean out the old cement as previously described and apply a coat of contact cement to the countertop and to the patch. Wait 10 minutes, until each surface is dry and lower the patch to the countertop. If you have been careful in the cutting operation the patch should be nearly invisible.

You can salvage the brush used for applying the contact cement by soaking it in a lacquer thinner, but no matter how well you clean the brush it will be useless for applying paint or varnish. You might as well use an inexpensive brush that can be discarded after use.

New Kitchen Window Sills

Of all the window sills in the house, the kitchen sills take the biggest beating. They are subject to sun, moisture from cooking and rain and the inevitable flowerpots. And no matter how often they are painted, they still tend to look somewhat shabby. Now that you have some experience with working with Formica, treat your kitchen window sills so that they will never — but never — require painting.

The first step is to trim off the rounded edge of the sill with a saw in order to obtain a flat vertical surface as Formica will not adhere to a sharply curved surface. Next, sand the surface with coarse sandpaper. Try to get down to the bare wood. Don't bother trying to get the surface too smooth — the contact cement will adhere better to a rough surface.

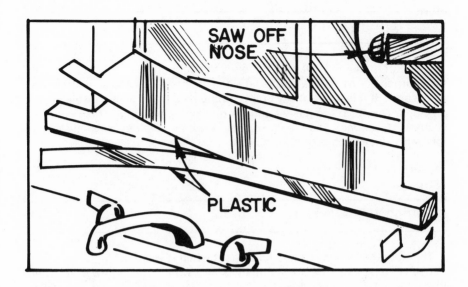

Measure and cut the Formica to fit. Cut it with the good side up if using a backsaw or a bench saw. The good side should be down, however, if you use a portable power saw. Now try the cut piece for a trial fit. Trim by filing if necessary.

Coat the window sill and the back of the Formica with contact cement. Keep the window open when applying the cement. Allow the cement to dry until it is not tacky (10 or 15 minutes). With a short window sill, 36 inches or less in length, a "slip sheet" is not necessary. With a longer sill, use the slip sheet to assure accuracy in placing the new piece on the sill. (see page 32 for slip sheet instructions.)

Do the same for the narrow front edge of the sill. After the cement has set, use a router, plane, or file to trim the Formica on the horizontal part of the sill flush with the vertical edge.

To assure good adhesion, go over the entire area with a padded block of wood and a mallet. Be especially attentive to the edges. If in doubt, it is a good idea to clamp the Formica overnight. Use C-clamps and protect the surface with scrap wood. Now you can forget window sill maintenance for the life of the house!

Loose Refrigerator Gaskets

That soft rubber or vinyl gasket around the door of the refrigerator is there for a purpose — to make a good seal when the door is closed so that no cold air escapes. If it is loose at any point, it should be glued back into place. Apply Super Glue-3 to the gasket and, as quickly as possible, press in place. Hold for 10 seconds and the loose gasket will be repaired. Use only a drop for every 2 linear inches of loose gasket.

Cleaning Vinyl Covered Furniture

That dinette set that looked so elegant when it was first installed in the kitchen can be made to look as fresh as new with a little elbow grease and Pizazz® vinyl and rubber dressing. First remove as much dirt and grease as you can with warm water and soap. Rinse everything off and dry with a clean cloth then cover the floor where you're working with newspaper.

Next apply Pizazz over all the vinyl parts of the chairs and table, paying particular attention to the seating areas. Don't be in a hurry to wipe it off — this product does a better job if allowed to soak in for a few hours. Then wipe off and buff with a soft cloth. Your family will be surprised at the "new" dinette set you just acquired.

Repairing Vinyl Tears

Of course if your vinyl furniture has a tear, repair it first before attempting to clean it. This is fairly simple. All you need is a tube of Clear Formula V® Vinyl Adhesive. It will repair most any product made of vinyl or leather.

First, examine the tear or damage on the vinyl. No doubt you have been looking at it for a long time and know exactly what it's like. Trim the edges of the tear with a nail scissors so they are clean, with no protruding bits of fabric. For a short tear or cut, apply the adhesive to the edges of the tear and butt the edges together. Then use masking tape to hold the edges together while the adhesive dries. It is best to keep the tape on for 12 hours by which time the maximum strength of the adhesive is developed. After removing the tape use fine sandpaper to remove excess adhesive. Do not use a solvent as this will weaken the joint.

How about large tears or cuts? The technique for repairing them is somewhat different. Cut a piece of cloth large enough to fit under the torn area. Brush the cloth with the adhesive and slip it under the area to be repaired. Carefully lift the torn or cut edges and apply some more cement on the under surface of the vinyl. About 1/4-inch width is enough. If necessary, use tape to keep the vinyl in place until the adhesive is dry. Again, use fine sandpaper to remove any excess and to smooth the seam.

The adhesive will dry in 40 minutes or so. It is best to leave your handiwork alone until the next morning when it will be safe to remove the tape and admire your "good-as-new" chair.

This adhesive is extremely flexible and can be safely used on vinyl — or leather — that is subject to compression such as chair and sofa seats; another feature — it dries clear.

Those Drip, Drip, Dripping Faucets

The faucets that are most apt to drip in the house are those in the kitchen. They are subject to more use, and therefore more wear than all of the other faucets in the house combined. It is for this reason that washerless faucets were first designed for kitchen use — and later for the lavatories in the bathrooms. But, most homes still have washer-type faucets — and they drip — and they require new washers from time to time.

So, let us go about eliminating faucets' drips. First turn off the water. A sink or lavatory may have a separate shut-off valve for the hot and cold water supply under the sink or bowl. If you can't find such a valve, turn off the main water supply. You will always find the shut-off valve very close to where the main water pipe enters the house.

All household faucets work on the same principle. As you turn a handle, a washer on the end of a threaded shaft presses against a seat to turn off the water. Determine just what type of faucet you have by consulting the drawings.

Type A

Sink, utility, boiler drain, or garden hose connection. After turning off the water, open the faucet handle (2) a couple of turns. Remove the packing nut (3) with an open end wrench by turning it counterclockwise. When the packing nut is off, you can remove the threaded stem (4) by turning the handle counterclockwise until the stem leaves the faucet body (7). Next, remove the washer (5) by unscrewing the small brass bolt (6) that holds the washer in place.

Replace it with a new washer of the same size and thickness. Install the washer with the rounded side facing the bottom of the faucet. In an emergency, you can try reversing the washer — it sometimes helps if you have no new washers on hand. If the brass bolt (6) is worn, replace it with a new brass bolt — never use a steel bolt.

Reassemble the faucet by inserting the threaded stem, screwing it down a few turns, then installing the packing nut. The packing nut should not be tightened at this point. Turn the faucet handle fully clockwise, so that it seats firmly. Now tighten the packing nut. If the handle does not turn freely, back off the packing nut 1/8 of a turn.

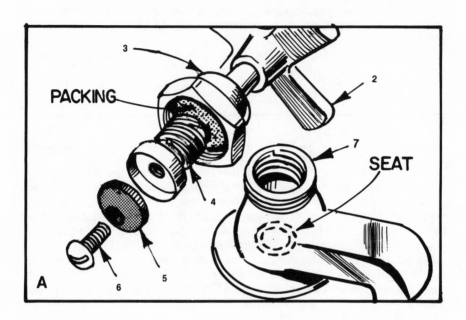

Type B

Generally used for kitchen sinks, has a swinging spout and mixes hot and cold water. The cold water faucet at the right has a left-hand thread. First turn off the water, open the faucet handle one or two turns, and remove the bolt that holds the handle in place (1). Next, pull off the handle. If it binds, tap it lightly with a block of wood while moving the handle back and forth. Now remove the bonnet (3). Wrap some tape around it so you can get a good grip with your fingers. If you must use a wrench to remove the bonnet, make sure that the wrench does not cut through the tape as the wrench is applied. The bonnet is unscrewed by turning it in a counterclockwise direction. Now apply a wrench to the stem assembly which projects out of the faucet body. Use an open end wrench that fits the stem assembly. Some stem assemblies have just two flat sides instead of being hexagonal in shape.

Turn the wrench counterclockwise to loosen the stem assembly. Use the faucet handle to remove the stem assembly (4) from the faucet body. Remove the small bolt (6) holding the washer (5) in place and replace with a new washer of the same size. If the brass bolt (6) shows signs of wear, replace with a brass bolt — do not use a steel bolt. If you have difficulty removing the brass bolt because the top is corroded and you cannot fit a screwdriver into the slot, cut a new or deeper slot with a hacksaw and then use the screwdriver again.

If you use a beveled washer, install it with the beveled or rounded side facing the seat of the faucet. Apply a little Vaseline to the threaded parts before assembling to make the job easier next time. Now install the stem assembly, and tighten securely with the wrench (the faucet should be in a half-open position to avoid binding). Install the bonnet, then the handle, and finally the bolt that holds the handle in place. Note that the handle is serrated to fit similar serrations in the stem of the faucet assembly. These serrations will allow you to replace the handle so that it points to eight o'clock if it is the hot water faucet and to four o'clock for the cold water side when both faucets are in the completely closed position. Now turn on the water.

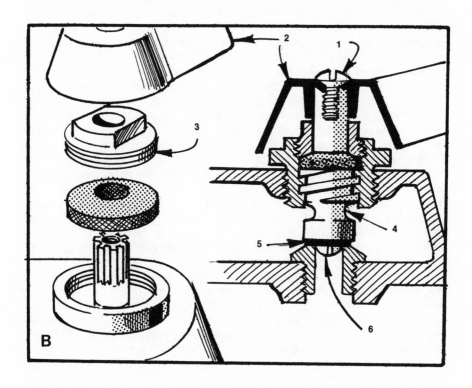

Type C

Generally found in bathroom sinks, rigid spout, mixes hot and cold water; both faucets, hot and cold, turn in the same direction. Turn off the water. Remove decorative cap (9) on top of the handle. You may have to use a pliers, so wrap it with tape to prevent scratching. Unscrewing the cap will expose a small brass bolt (2). This bolt may have a crossed slot, in which case you will need a Phillips screwdriver to remove it.

Next, remove the handle by pulling it upwards. If it binds, tap it with a block of wood or screwdriver handle, moving the handle back and forth at the same time. Then remove the decorative bonnet (8), wrapped with tape for a good grip. You should be able to unscrew it with your fingers, but if a wrench is required, make sure the wrench does not cut through the tape and scratch the finish. Removing the bonnet will expose the faucet stem (4).

Two nuts will be visible (4a, 4b). The upper one is a packing nut and need not be touched. With an open-end wrench turn the lower nut (4b) in a counterclockwise direction until the entire faucet stem (4) can be removed from the faucet body (7). The lower half of the faucet stem (4c) is unscrewed to expose the washer (5). This lower half also contains the seat against which the washer bears. The seat in this type of faucet is in the stem assembly and not in the faucet body. Unscrew the faucet washer bolt (6) and replace with a new washer (5).

Before assembling, apply a little Vaseline or white lubricant to all threaded parts to ease the job next time. Reassemble the faucet by installing the stem into the faucet body and tighten the lower nut (4b). Try the faucet before installing the bonnet. If water leaks past the stem, tighten the packing nut. If the handle turns too hard, back off the packing nut (4a) 1/8th turn. Now remove the handle, screw down the bonnet, then install the handle again (don't forget the small locking bolt) and finally the decorative cap. Now turn on the water.

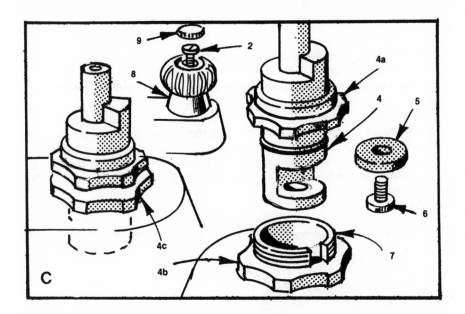

C

Type D

Tub and shower faucets. Turn off the water supply. Unscrew the small bolt (1) from the face of the handle (2). Remove the handle by pulling it straight out. If it won't budge, tap it with a block of wood while at the same time turning it back and forth.

Next, remove the bonnet (3) by unscrewing the circular retaining nut (3a). Use tape to protect the finish as you will need pliers to remove this nut. The valve stem assembly will now be exposed, but you will need a special wrench to remove it as it is recessed into the wall. You can get it at any large hardware store, they resemble automobile sparkplug wrenches. A set, complete with handle, is a good investment. Squirt a little penetrating lubricant around the threads.

Apply the wrench to the larger of the two exposed nuts (3b). The smaller nut (3c) is a packing nut which need not be disturbed. Turn the wrench counterclockwise until the entire stem assembly (4) can be removed from the inside of the faucet. Note that the lower half of the stem assembly (4c) can be unscrewed to expose the washer. Sometimes this lower half will remain in the faucet body — just fish it out with your finger, it's a loose fit within the faucet body.

The seat in this type of faucet is in the stem assembly and not in the faucet body. Unscrew the small bolt (6) holding the washer (5) in place and replace with a new washer of the same size. If the brass bolt is corroded, replace with a new brass bolt. Before assembling, apply a little Vaseline or other lubricant to all threaded parts to ease the job next time. Reassembly the faucet by installing the stem assembly in the faucet body. Tighten the large nut (3b) with the special wrench. The packing nut (3c) should be tightened if it is loose.

Try the faucet before installing the bonnet. If water leaks past the stem, tighten the packing nut (3c) a bit more. If the handle turns too tightly, back off the packing nut 1/8th turn. Remove the handle, install the bonnet, replace the circular retaining nut (3a) and finally the small bolt (1) that holds the handle in place.

The faucet bonnets on shower and tub fixtures must always be removed to expose the faucet stems. They can be held in place with a setscrew, a circular nut, or a hex nut, which must be unscrewed first before the bonnet can be removed. Some bonnets, (such as Type B and C) are unscrewed from the faucet assembly.

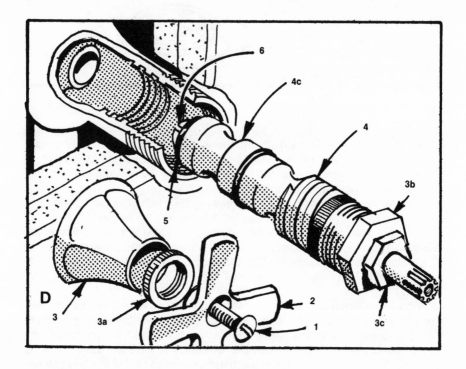

The drawings illustrate the most popular types of washerless faucets.

Emergency Washer Replacement

Sometimes you may find that it is impossible to remove the brass screw that holds the faucet washer in place. In fact, there may not be any brass screw at all as it has corroded and disappeared with age (yes, brass can and does corrode). What can you do? If you have extra brass screws on hand, you can tap and drill for a new screw (it's really a bolt) — but only if you have a tap and drill set.

There is a much simpler remedy. Clean the washer seat, select the appropriate washer and apply just a single drop of Super Glue-3 to the washer. Spread it around with a matchstick and immediately install the washer in its recess. Press, to assure a good bond — and that's all there is to it. The washer will stay put without benefit of a single brass screw.

If your faucet still leaks after you have installed a new washer, the chances are that the faucet seat is badly scored and should be dressed or replaced. A kit for dressing and renewing a faucet seat is available for less than a dollar. A small cutter at the end of a shaft is inserted into the faucet body and turned back and forth until the seat is smooth. Some faucets have replaceable seats. They are made of brass and look like a Lifesaver candy with a square hole. A new seat costs about 35c and can be installed with a special square shank tool — or in a pinch, with a screwdriver that fits the diagonal of the square opening.

Washerless and Single Control Faucets

First introduced for kitchen use, they are now available for the bathroom as well. The most important feature, of course, is their lack of conventional washers, and therefore the need for constant replacement. But after a few years of use, even washerless faucets need attention — they too can leak.

In the washerless faucets, the flow of water is controlled by a valve instead of a washer pressing against a seat. This valve may be a sliding, tipping or rotating valve (it's a tipping valve in single control, washerless faucets).

When washerless faucets were first introduced, each manufacturer had his own design for the operation of his particular faucet — and, more important, the type of replacement needed when a leak did develop. Today, manufacturers have standardized on two or three types and replacement is less of a headache, but the replacement still must be the proper type. Parts for different makes are not interchangeable.

The replacement part (ball or cartridge style) is available from hardware stores and from plumbing supply stores. After procuring the proper replacement valve (give the dealer the name and model number of the faucet) you can proceed to make the replacement.

First turn off the water. Then pry off or unscrew the index button on top of the faucet, unscrew the bonnet and pull the exposed stem up and out. Now all you need to do is to remove the old valve seat assembly and replace it with the new one. Replace the stem, bonnet, and index button, and the job is done.

If a leak occurs at the spout where it swings, then new O rings are called for. To do this job, the spout nut is removed and the spout lifted out by rotating it back and forth gently. Cut the old O ring and stretch the new O ring over the post and roll it into the groove. Replace the spout and the spout nut. When replacing the parts, always apply a little grease to the moving parts.

Chapter 5

THE DINING ROOM

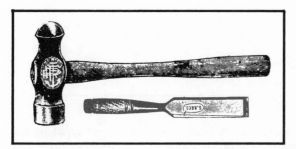

Fixing Furniture Scratches

From the kitchen it is only a step or two to the dining room. What are you going to do with that deep scratch on your lovely dining room table? Filling in the scratch with a plastic wood filling material gives you excellent results.

The area that requires filling should be thoroughly cleaned — no old wax or polish should be in the crevice. Score the inside with the tip of a penknife or a bit of folded sandpaper. This is necessary in order to give the filler a "bite." Next squeeze out the filler into the crack or the scratch. If the scratch is deep, fill it with more than one layer, allowing each layer to dry before applying the next. Build up the repaired area flush with the surrounding surface. If it is a little higher, it will have to be trimmed by scraping it down with a knife or a razor blade. Don't use sandpaper as it may scratch the adjacent area.

If the wood filler as it comes from the tube matches the rest of the wood, that's fine. If it doesn't, use the colored "matchsticks" (pencils of staining compound), to get the exact color needed. The stain should be applied only after the wood filler is dry. Don't be afraid to experiment. You may use a combination of two matchsticks to get the required color.

After completing this part of the operation, polish the entire surface with a good grade of paste wax. The matchsticks, incidentally, can be used alone to fill small holes and minute scratches.

Treating Sticking Drawers

Drawers that slide in and out with difficulty may be sticking because of a lack of lubrication along the runners. Remove a hard-to-budge drawer from the desk or bureau and examine its construction. It probably has a groove on each side which engages two parallel cleats in the furniture; or has two cleats which engage matching cutouts in the furniture; or merely rides on the bottom opening of the drawer. Examine the drawer to see where it is binding. You should look for an especially shiny or worn area on one or both sides of the drawer. Apply a little white lubricant to that particular area and your problem should be over.

If the drawer still sticks, a bit more drastic measure is called for — sanding or planing down the offending area. Use coarse sandpaper for fast wood removal, followed by fine sandpaper.

If a large amount of wood is to be removed, it should be done with a plane. Clamp the drawer on the workbench with a couple of C clamps and then use the plane — but sparingly. Try the drawer for fit after just a few shavings have been removed.

All of the foregoing applies to drawers that have a "lipped" construction. That is a type of drawer that has a wide lip in front that completely covers the opening into which the drawer slides.

Other drawers, usually found in better grades of furniture, have a "flush" fit. The entire front of the drawer fits completely into its opening — top, bottom and sides. Sticking in this type of drawer is most always on some part of the front area. Sanding or light planing will usually cure the trouble. The exposed raw wood can then be treated with wood filler and wax stain to prevent warping.

Drawers that stick due to swollen wood (if the house hasn't been occupied for ages and there's been no heat) can be cured with a little heat. Put a 50-watt lamp in a trouble light and place it in the drawer over an asbestos flatiron pad. Keep it on for a few hours, checking frequently to avoid possible scorching. The wood should shrink and the drawer slide smoothly again.

Really Stuck Drawers

There are drawers that simply can't be opened because a knife or a fork has become jammed into the top of the drawer. Swearing and stamping your feet will obviously not help, so first try jiggling the drawer as much as you are able, and pulling the drawer in and out. This may settle the contents, but it may not help. (Drawers are perverse creatures like many other so-called inanimate objects that harass man.) Next try pounding the drawer from the bottom. This to may settle its "stomach." If not, try tipping over the furniture — with its obstinate drawer — in the hope that some sort of new displacement will occur enabling the drawer to change its mind — and its contents.

If this doesn't work, get a carving knife (the long old-fashioned kind in vogue before the day of electric carving knives). Insert the tip in the opening at the top of the drawer as far as possible and move the knife left to right until you can feel it engage the obstruction. Keep moving the knife while at the same time tugging at the drawer. The chances are your ingenuity has solved the problem and the drawer can now be opened without any difficulty. This method only works on flush drawers, though, and not on the lipped type.

Sticking Doors

A sticking door is closely related to a sticking drawer. But don't do any sanding or planing until you have checked the hinges. Make sure that the hinges at the top and bottom of the door are securely fastened to the door jamb as well as to the door. Check each screw; is it tight in its recess? Tighten all the screws.

STUCK DOORS

PLUG FILLS LOOSE SCREW HOLES

If any screw keeps turning as you tighten it, then it needs attention. Withdraw it completely and insert an epoxy glue-moistened plug into the hole — a wooden matchstick will do in a pinch. Reinsert the screw. Now it won't keep on turning after it is seated.

Loose hinges are the chief cause of sticking doors. Well, all right, you have tightened all the hinges and the door still sticks. Then you may have to sand the area that sticks. Slide a sheet of typing paper between the door stop and the door. Notice where the paper refuses to go any further. That is the place where sticking is occurring. Mark it. If the sticking part is somewhere in the middle of the door, the top, or not too near the bottom, you are in luck as you will not have to remove the door from its hinges. First try sanding the binding part. Work at it for a few minutes and then see if the bind has disappeared. Try again. If it still binds, a more drastic method must be employed — planing. Open the door and place a wedge under it so it will be immobilized. Now remove a few shavings of wood with the plane, check the door, and plane again if necessary. This treatment may complete the job. But suppose the bind is at the bottom of the door, dragging across the saddle. In this case, you have no recourse but to remove the door. You need not remove the hinges; just drive out the pins that hold the hinges together and the door will slip out of its moorings.

An assistant may be necessary at this point to hold the door steady while you apply your muscles and a plane to the bottom edge of the door. Examine the door to determine where the bind occurs. (The wood will appear shiny at that spot.) Plane away this part first and then continue to remove some stock from the rest of the bottom — just be on the safe side.

Of course, if new carpeting has been installed and it is just impossible to close the door because of the thickness of the new carpeting, something more than planing may be necessary. You'll need to cut 1/2-inch or so from the bottom of the door with a saw.

It's best to do this job with a power saw — but a hand saw will also do the job with a little more time and muscle invested. Set the door on a couple of carpenter's horses or across two chairs. Clamp a narrow board or a 2 × 4 along the width of the board to serve as a guide for sawing. If you have a power saw, you will have to make an allowance for the width of the base of the saw before clamping the guide in place. If you are going to do the job with a hand saw, clamp the board so that the pencil line indicating the cut is just visible. Saw along this line. After finishing the cut, lightly sand each side of the cut.

The next step is to reinstall the door — and here again you may need some help. Guide the door into the jamb so that the lower hinge halves engage. Then push the door to engage the upper hinge halves. An assistant is welcome at this point to hold the bottom of the door to prevent it from leaving the lower hinge while you are aiming for the upper hinge. It sounds tricky, but it can done. When the door is in place, have the assistant hold the door as you drive in the hinge pins. And incidentally before you install the hinge pins, coat them with a light grease such as Vaseline. This treatment will allow the door to swing freely and will positively eliminate ghostlike squeaks.

Tightening Chair Rungs

How about those dining room chairs? Are they loose and wobbly? If so, take a look at the rungs of the chairs. More lthan likely they are loose in their sockets. The repair is a simple one. Turn the chair upside down and remove the loose rung from its socket. This can be done by gently stretching the opposite side of the chair.

Scrape out all dried glue from inside the socket and around the end of the rung. Use sandpaper for the final cleanup. Gluing is the next step, but before you do so, get a length of stout cord (clothesline will do) and a couple of sticks — one about 6 inches long — the other about 2 feet long. Coat the end of the chair rung with household cement and insert it into the socket. Now tie the two opposite legs together with the clothesline, insert the short stick between the clothesline and turn it end to end to force the two legs together, thus assuring a good glue bond. Use the second stick as an anchor to prevent the "tourniquet" from unraveling.

This type of operation is known as a Spanish windlass and is a sure-fire method of repairing loose chair rungs (see drawing for details). The cement dries clear, but any excess can be removed before it has dried with a bit of cotton and nail polish remover.

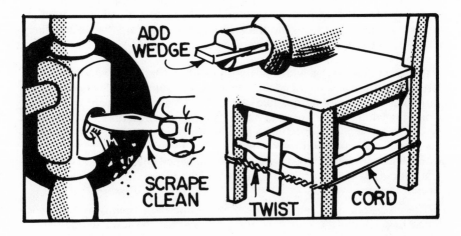

Eliminating Floor Squeaks

Floor squeaks are apt to develop at those areas subject to the most foot traffic — at doorways and sometimes around and near the center of the room, but seldom near the wall — people don't walk there.

It's a good idea to get rid of these offending noises — a frequent problem in new homes as well as old. If you can get at the underside of the floor in the basement or cellar, you can effect a temporary repair by driving several nails between the floor boards and the joists as shown. Do not use wedges as some so-called "experts" recommend. Wedges will only raise the floor boards in the room above.

For a more permanent repair locate the position of each floor joist in the room above by drilling small holes on each side of the joists. Then drive a series of annular ring or screw-type nails in the middle of each floor board. It is best to drill a pilot hole if the floor boards are of oak or a similar tough hardwood which may be subject to splitting.

If the floors above are covered with floor covering such as tiles or carpeting, and you have no great desire to rip them up, try this technique: drill clearance holes — no more than 3/4-inch deep — in the rough flooring, from below, and small pilot holes in the finished flooring. Be careful that the pilot holes do not penetrate the finished flooring. This method, of course, only works if the floor is exposed in the basement.

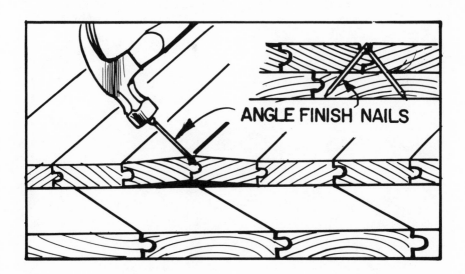

ANGLE FINISH NAILS

For squeaking floors on upper floors, remove any carpeting and locate the floor joists (they always run at right angles to the long side of the room) by tapping the floor with the handle of a hammer. A slightly deadened sound will indicate the location of the joists. Then drive ring-type or screw-type nails in the middle of each floor board. A good method to follow in locating all those irritating squeaks is to walk around the room and mark with chalk every spot where a squeak occurs.

Chapter 6

THE LIVING ROOM

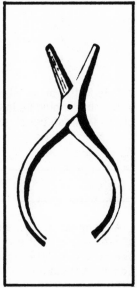

This is the place where we spend our leisure time at home, and where everything should be in working order. Let us take a look at some of the problems that can beset us in our sanctum sanctorum.

The Lamps

Are any lamps flickering? This may be due to a loose connection in the socket, a lamp not firmly screwed into its socket, faulty extension cords, defective outlet, or loose wire nuts. Let's take them in order.

Loose Connection In Socket

First, unplug the cord (if it is a floor lamp) and remove the shade and harp from the lamp. Take the socket apart by pressing firmly at the side — the spot is sometimes marked *Press* — and at the same time pulling the top part from the bottom. This now exposes the innards of the socket.

Check the screws that hold the two wires in place. Even if they do not appear to be loose, tighten them with a screwdriver. Just to be on the safe side, wrap a piece of adhesive tape around the screws; this will serve as an additional safeguard in case the paper insulation of the socket should fail due to age and heat. Now replace the brass shell of the socket, making sure it clicks into place.

Loose Lamp

Always unplug the cord before you start to work. The obvious thing here is to screw the lamp deeper into the socket, but sometimes this does not help. The reason is that the contact in the center of the socket may have been pushed so far down that it is not touching the bulb. Use a nut pick to pry it up slightly — that's all that is required.

Faulty Extension Cord

Extension cords should never really be used around the house except in emergencies, or when using a power tool outdoors or lighting up the attic for an insulation job. But they are available, they are sold, and they are used.

Check to see that the connections at the female and male ends are good and tight. Tug on the cord at either end. Any flickering is a sure sign that the connections are at fault and should be checked. If the extension has a molded plug at either end, the only recourse is to cut off the defective plug about 2 inches from the end to make sure that any chafed or broken wire is also removed. Tie a knot in the wire, as indicated in the drawing, and scrape off about 1/2-inch of insulation from each wire. Twist the strands of the wire together and loop each wire around the binding screw of the new plug. The loop should be in a clockwise direction so that as the screws are tightened, the wire will not "walk" away from under the heads of the screws.

There are no bare wires visible in an extension cord with molded plugs. You can have the same result using E-Pox-E ribbon. Cut off an inch or so, knead it between your fingers, and when it is a uniform color push it into the open areas of the plug; it will make a *super safe* insulating seal.

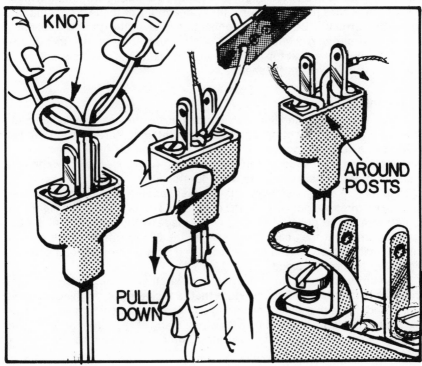

Defective Outlet

This is a rare occurence, but it can happen, especially if the outlet has been overloaded at times and plugs are removed from it without first turning off the switch. The first thing to do is to determine just what fuse or circuit breaker controls the current to that outlet. If you're working by yourself, plug a radio in the outlet, turn up the volume, and standing at the fusebox, remove one fuse at a time until the radio stops playing.

When you have found the right fuse, (or circuit breaker) unscrew it completely and go back to the outlet. Remove the screw from the middle of the cover plate and remove the plate; next remove the two screws, one at the top and one at the bottom of the "receptacle" (the professional term for an outlet). Gently pull on the outlet to remove it from its metal box; it will still be connected to the wires. Once you've removed the screws that hold the wires in place, you can remove the defective outlet from its box.

When you install the new outlet *make sure it is the grounding type* (now required by law in all new work). This type of outlet has three openings for the plug; the U-shaped opening, is the ground connection. Install the new outlet by connecting the black wire to the brass binding post and the white wire to the nickle-plated binding post. Now you will notice a third screw, painted green. This is the ground connection which carries no current.

If your home is wired with BX cable, then the outlet is automatically grounded as it is installed and no attention need be paid to the green screw. However, if your home is wired with Romex, the green screw should be connected by means of a short length of wire called a pigtail, either to the metal box (the new ones have a screw for the connection), or to the grounding wire in the Romex cable. Be sure this connection goes to the ground wire, *not to the current carrying white or black wires.* Push the outlet into the box, install the two screws at top and bottom, and install the cover plate. Turn on the current, and you are finished.

Loose Wire Nuts

A mysterious flickering light can sometimes be due to a loose connection in a switch or in the junction box that feeds that light. Wire nuts are used by electricians to make connections. At one time all electrical connections were soldered and taped, but in our headlong rush for efficiency and less work for more money, wire nuts were developed.

They look like tiny thimbles with a metal spiral core and a thick plastic cover. The wires are pushed into the core, the cover is twisted in a clockwise direction and the connection is quickly made without benefit of solder, tape, or time. But they can work loose — the 60 cycle hum of the electric current can loosen wire nuts, especially if they have not been properly tightened in the first place.

Open up the cover plate of the nearest switch or junction box and check the wire nuts. If it is a ceiling fixture that is flickering, drop the decorative half-round cover that hides the wiring and check the connections. Be sure the switch is off before fiddling with wires. If any of the wire nuts are loose, tighten them, and as a further safeguard, wrap some tape around them so they will not loosen in the future.

Installing Switches

There are times when it is inconvenient and perhaps even hazardous to have to walk over to a lamp in order to light it. Let us first consider the installation of a single switch that controls only one lamp.

Wall Switches

Turn off the current going to the ceiling light by removing the fuse or flipping the circuit breaker to *Off.* Next, determine where you want the switch located. A wall switch should always be on the doorknob side of the wall, about four feet from the floor. Tap the wall to locate the studs, or drill a series of 1/16-inch holes to find the stud. Trace the outline of the metal box that will house the switch on the wall so that one side will be next to a stud. Drill a hole in each corner and use a keyhole saw to cut away the plaster.

Next, you will have to pass a cable (BX or Romex) long enough to reach from the light to the switch position. To do this you will need a brace, a long bit, and an electrician's snake. Drill the holes as shown in the drawing to pass the cable. Fish for the cable with the snake. Insert one end of the cable through one of the knockouts in the ceiling box after removing about five inches of the protective covering to expose the two wires. Strip off an inch of insulation from each wire. Disconnect the black wire to the ceiling light, and connect it to the black wire of the new cable. The white wire of the new cable goes to the ceiling light connection from which the black wire was removed. Solder and tape the connections, or use wire nuts. Note that the white wire from the fuse box to the ceiling light is not disturbed.

Now go back to the opening in the wall for the switch. Push the cable back into the opening and try the switch box for fit. The box should rest against the side of the wall stud. Remove the box and drill two holes in the side of the box for mounting. Make the pilot holes for the screws with an awl bent to a right angle, or you can use a red hot nail also bent to a right angle and gripped with a pair of locking pliers.

Pass the cable through one of the knockouts and clamp it in place after first removing about five inches of the protective covering. Strip off an inch of insulation from each wire. Now push the box back into the opening and secure it to the wall with two roundhead Phillips screws and an offset screwdriver.

Connect the two wires to the switch terminals. Fold the excess wire behind the switch, and gently force the switch into the box. Secure the switch to the box with the two screws supplied, and then install the cover plate. The cover plate should hide the opening cut in the plaster wall. If it doesn't, patch the hole with plaster. Now replace the fuse (or circuit breaker) and try the switch. It works!

Replacing a defective switch

The first step is to flip off the circuit breaker or remove the fuse that controls the circuit to the defective switch. Next, remove the cover plate by unscrewing its two screws. This will expose the switch. Remove the top and bottom screws that hold the switch in the box. Gently pull out the switch to expose the two screws that connect the wires to the switch.

Note that one wire is black (or red) and the second wire is white but probably painted black at the end. This is a legal requirement as all "hot" wires must be black or painted black. Loosen the two screws holding the wires in place so you can remove the switch.

Do not tamper with any other wires you may find in the box except those connected to the switch. These wires may feed other lights or outlets and have nothing to do with the switch you're working on. When you install the new switch, connect it in the same way as the old one. Make sure the switch will be in the *Off* position when the toggle is down.

If you replace the defective switch with a silent mercury-type switch, look for the word TOP stamped on the switch body and install with this end up top. When you make the wire connections, wrap the wires around the binding posts in a clockwise direction so that tightening the screws will keep the wires wrapped around the shank of the screws.

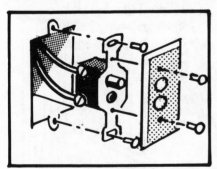 

Three-way switches

Three-way switches are used to control the same light from two different locations. They can be located at any convenient place; at the foot of a stairway in order to light up the hallway above, for instance, and then a second switch to turn off the light at the upper landing. Replacement of these switches is the same as for conventional switches except that they have three connections instead of two — usually one wire at the top of the switch and two at the bottom. Mark the wires so you will know to which screw they go before removing them. If the replacement is a mercury-type switch, install it with the word TOP at the top. (See drawing for details.)

Unlike conventional switches, the position of the toggle on three-way switches does not necessarily mean the light is *On* when the toggle is up, or *Off* when the toggle is down. The *On* and *Off* positions of either switch depend upon the *On* and *Off* positions of the other switch.

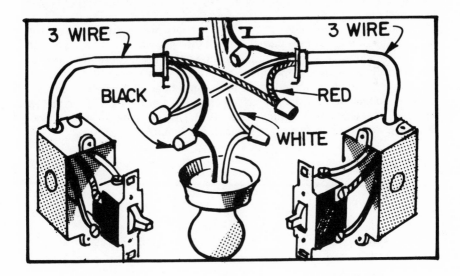

Securing Scatter Rugs

Having tripped on a scatter rug more than once, and scattered the contents of my tray, it is my firm conviction that this kind of rug received its name because of the scattering it causes.

Such accidents can be eliminated by treating scatter rugs so they are slipproof. All you need is a few dabs of clear silicone sealer applied to the back of the rug. Each spot should be about as big as a silver dollar and spaced around the periphery of the rug with a few spots in the center.

But here is the trick! Allow the silicone sealer to dry overnight, facing up. You are not cementing the rug to the floor; you are merely applying a skidproof surface to the back of the rug. The next morning, place the rug back at the scene of the previous accidents and that's it. No more slipping.

If you are after a more permanent installation, apply a dab of the sealer to the floor directly under the sealer on the rug and press down by walking on the rug.

Preventing Carpet Raveling

While we are on the subject of rugs and carpets, have you ever had to trim a large rug to fit a smaller room? The problem that arises is what to do with the raw edges of the rug after trimming. The rug that comes from the factory has either a woven selvage, or a tape sewn to the edge of the carpet to prevent raveling.

To reconstruct the edge, you can either laboriously sew a new tape around the raw edges of the carpet, or do it the easy way, by applying a bead of adhesive along the edges. Lift up the rug so that the edge of the carpet to be treated is in a vertical position; prop it up with a couple of chairs if necessary. Then all you need to do is to run a bead of household cement (you'll need several tubes) all along the cut edge. Let the cement dry; a few hours will do. This cement will adhere to any type of carpet — wool, nylon, or acrylic — and dries to a clear, transparent finish.

Chapter 7

COVERING WALLS

In medieval days, most people covered their walls with a form of whitewash — except for nobles, who could afford tapestries. We are fortunate today to have many choices available to us to fit all tastes and budgets.

Installing Wall Panels

Sold on paneling? A beautifully paneled room is one of the most satisfying home improvement projects you can undertake.

The first thing to do is to measure the height and width of the walls you are planning to cover, with allowance for windows and doors. Measure for crown molding (where the panels will meet the ceiling) and baseboard for the floor. You will also need molding for areas around windows, doors and corners. Next, visit your lumber dealer and make your selection. Most panels come in 4 × 8 foot sizes, though 10 foot lengths are also available. Store the panels in the room where the job is to take place for at least 24 hours beforehand.

In the meantime, get the room ready. Remove all furniture, any molding at top and bottom, and all outlet and switch plates. Begin at the most inconspicuous part of the room, so that you will have become an expert by the time you reach the end! Make sure the first panel is perpendicular (plumb) to the floor. If necessary, cut the panels so that they are an inch shorter than the wall height. The 1/2-inch space at top and bottom will be covered by molding.

Panels can be installed over plaster or dry walls in good condition by cementing them in place. Apply parallel rows of cement (it comes in a tube, like a caulking cartridge) every 4-inches to the back of the panel. Rest the cemented panel on a couple of 1/2-inch thick blocks of wood at the bottom for supports and press it against the wall.

Drive four nails along the top edge to act as a hinge, pull the panel away from the wall and insert a block between the wall and the panel to give the cement a chance to set — 10 minutes should be enough. Remove the block of wood and press the panel back to the wall. To make certain of good adhesion, pound the panel with a hammer and a block of wood wrapped in a towel. Start at top and work your way down. This is good insurance and worth the extra time.

The edges of the panel should be nailed with small brads every 6-inches. Drive them below the surface of the wood with a nail set and fill the holes with plastic wood filler. The Furniture Touch-Up Kit has 4 pencil-like staining compounds to match the color of most woods. Continue paneling until you come to the first door opening or window.

An easy way to cut a panel for an exact fit around the door or window is to make a pattern out of corrugated cardboard. Cut the cardboard to fit the opening, lay it over the panel, then mark and cut accordingly.

When cutting a panel, cut with the good side up to prevent splintering. As added insurance apply a strip of tape along the cutting line.

Openings for switches and outlets are easily located by taping carbon paper over the opening. Place the panel against the wall and pound it with your fist to mark the back of the panel. Drill a 1/4-inch hole in each corner and use a coping saw or jigsaw to make the required opening. Now apply the cement and install the panel.

Since the raw edge of the panel will be exposed when you cut to fit a window opening, use cap molding to hide the edges. Cap molding is made to match most panel finishes, and adds a professional touch to the job.

After the entire room has been paneled (or only one or two walls, if you prefer), the next step is to apply the crown molding at the top. Stain and finish it to match the paneling. The molding should be mitered or coped at all corners. Use 2-inch brads to nail the molding through the paneling and into the wall. Sink the brads below the surface and fill the holes with the filler. The same technique is used to install the baseboard molding where the paneling meets the floor.

Basement Paneling

Paneling a basement requires a somewhat different technique. First of all, walls are usually concrete or block construction and secondly, dampness is a factor. The first step is to make certain the walls to be paneled are impervious to water seepage. If necessary, coat the walls with a waterproofing cement paint (See Chapter 2).

BASEMENT PANELING

1 X 2" FURRING IN ADHESIVE OR NAILED

6"
16"
16"
16"

POLYETHYLENE VAPOR BARRIER

TWO WAYS TO NAIL

Next, nail 1 × 2-inch furring strips to the wall every 16-inches on centers. If the wall is uneven, shim or wedge the furring strips as required. Because dampness may still be a factor despite your best efforts to control it, back prime the panels with a sealer, such as shellac. Coat the reverse side of the panels, not the front.

The panels can be cemented or nailed to the furring strips, but nailing is simpler and faster than cementing. Use 1-inch brads and place the nails in the panel grooves. You will find a nailing groove every 16 inches, even though they appear to be at random intervals.

Flush panels without grooves must be cemented in place. To permit circulation of air behind the panels, use a special crown and baseboard molding that has slits in it for ventilation. If you use conventional molding, keep it 1/4-inch away from floor and ceiling to permit air movement. You may not want to use cap molding as it only comes in one style — round — but you can use any other type of molding that suits your fancy. Molding can be installed without nailing up using contact cement. Gluing the molding is much easier since nailing and setting the nails, on curved molding can be rather tricky.

Apply the contact cement to the area where the molding is to go and do the same to the back of the molding. Wait until the cement is no longer tacky — about 15 minutes — and attach. Start at the top and keep lowering the molding into place. Molding in long strips is quite flexible and you should have no trouble installing it. Pound it lightly with your fist along its entire length to make sure absolute contact is achieved from bottom to top.

Wallpapering

The first stop in wallpapering may be the most difficult of all — getting the whole family to agree on the pattern. Once you have made an irrevocable decision and are ready to paper, start by moving all the furniture to the center of the room, leaving plenty of working area for the job. Prepare the walls by patching all holes and cracks with a spackling compound and seal the patched parts with a thin coat of shellac. Even though you can paper over old wallpaper (provided there are no loose areas), it is best to remove old paper by soaking it with a removal preparation and then scraping it off. Sand the wall to remove any nicks that may have been made by the scraper.

Buy sufficient rolls of paper to cover the room; consult the table (See chart estimating wallpaper requirements on page 97.) Actually, most "wallpaper" is now made of vinyl with a cloth or paper backing and comes in rolls that are 27 inches wide. Manufacturers now call their products wallcoverings, not paper.

Start at a wall that has the fewest window and door openings and measure off a distance that is 1 inch less than the wallcovering width (26 inches, for instance). Suspend a plumb line at this point and snap a chalk line on the wall. This chalk line is most important as it will determine the "straightness" of the first strip and of all succeeding strips.

The next step is to mix the paste. Use a pail and keep stirring as you add the powder to water. A special paste must be used to hang the heavy vinyl wallcoverings that come in 54-inch widths. Keep adding the powder to the water, stirring all the time until the paste has the consistency of sour cream. Break up all lumps with your fingers or strain the paste through some cheesecloth.

Cut several strips of paper or wallcovering equal to the height of the wall you are going to cover, *plus* an overlap of 3-inches for the top and 3-inches for the bottom. Apply the paste to the back of the paper with a wide brush, paying particular attention to the edges of the paper. An unpasted area will show up as a blister on the wall.

Newspapers placed under the paper will keep your pasting table clean. If your table is too short to support a full length of paper, use a chair or a stool to hold the paper at either end to prevent creasing. Paste up half a length of paper (if your table is a short one) and fold up this half to meet the middle of the strip. Do not crease the fold. Do the same thing with the other half and now fold both halves together. The paper is folded paste side to paste side and can be handled easily by the dry, pattern side.

Line up the strip with the chalk line, leaving the 3-inch overlap at the ceiling. Unfold the paper, letting it drop free, and then carefully position the paper so that it lines up with the chalk line from top to bottom. Use a wide paperhanger's brush to force the paper into the corner of the room.

You will wind up with a 1/2-inch overlap into the adjacent corner wall as the paper was lined up at a distance of 26-1/2-inches from the corner, not the full 27-inch paper width. Apply the brush firmly over the entire surface of the paper, starting from the middle and working towards the edges. Make sure you have a good bond at the ceiling, baseboard, and along the edge.

Now cut and paste up the next strip. If the paper has a pattern that must be matched, you will have to make an allowance for it when you cut the paper. (Professional paper hangers will cut and paste up 1/2 dozen or more strips at a time!) Bring the second strip over and carefully butt it to the preceeding strip. Ease it in place by using the palms of your hands. Again use the brush to smooth out the paper. Wipe away any excess paste that oozes out between the seams with a sponge dampened with water. Use a seam roller to press down the seams. Press lightly with the roller to prevent the pattern of the wheel from being embossed on the paper.

Continue this way working around the room. Do not skip any problem areas with the expectation of coming back to them later. When you come to a switch plate or outlet, apply the paper right over it — after first removing the cover plate — and use a sharp knife to cut away the paper over the opening. Replace the cover plate after you have finished the entire papering job.

When you come to a fireplace, mantelpiece, window, or door, remove as much as possible of the waste paper before smoothing it in place. You can do an exact trimming job around these obstructions if you crease a line with a putty knife on the paper following the outline of the window, door, etc. Then cut along this line with a pair of scissors and finish by pressing the paper into place with your fingers, followed by the brush. Trimming away the excess at the ceiling and baseboard can be done with a sharp trimming knife as these are fairly long, straight cuts.

How about a recessed window? Paper the inside first, top and both sides, leaving an inch overlap on the walls all around. Then continue papering the walls and covering the overlap.

If you want to paper a ceiling, do this job first and apply the paper across the short side of the ceiling, not the long side. Leave an overlap of an inch or so to extend down the walls. This overlap is then covered when the walls are papered.

When papering a ceiling, bear in mind that some patterns cannot go up one wall, across the ceiling, and down the other wall, because of a definite correct side up pattern such as some flowers, faces, figures, and animals. In such a case, make sure the pattern on the walls faces right side up, while the ceiling pattern can go either way.

Chart for Estimating Wallpaper Requirements				
Distance around room in feet	Single rolls required when ceiling is:			Single rolls for ceiling
	8 ft.	9 ft.	10 ft.	
30	8	8	10	2
34	10	10	12	4
38	10	12	12	4
42	12	12	14	4
46	12	14	14	6
50	14	14	16	6
54	14	16	18	6
58	16	16	18	8
62	16	18	20	8
66	18	20	20	10
70	18	20	22	10
74	20	22	22	12
78	20	22	24	14
82	22	24	26	14
86	22	24	26	16
90	24	26	28	18

Note: Wallpaper is sold in single, double, and triple rolls. A single roll covers 30 square feet. Deduct a single roll for every two doors or windows of average size.

All About Painting

Painting is 90% preparation and cleanup, and only 10% of your time is spent moving the brush around. So it is fairly obvious that the finish — no matter what type of paint, varnish, or lacquer you are working with — depends upon how carefully the surface was prepared before the brush is dipped into the can.

Interior Painting

Paint is still the Number One finish. More surfaces are covered with paint than with all other types of finishes combined. In recent years there has been a virtual revolution in the paint industry. There are paints that can be thinned with water; paints that dry with a speckled finish; paints that are mixed with a hardener to make an epoxy finish; and paints that dry with a metallic finish. These are just a few of the many different paints on the market.

Latex, or water-thinned paints are most popular with homeowners. They have many qualities to recommend them: they dry in an hour, ready for a second coat; they have good covering qualities; brushes and rollers can be cleaned with water and soap. Any disadvantages? Yes, a few. At present you cannot get a high-gloss latex enamel in all colors; the actual thickness of a latex coat of paint is thinner than a comparable coat of an oil-based paint.

However, since a second coat can be applied within an hour, there is no excuse for waiting. Latex paints are now available for exterior use on clapboard and trim, and because of their water-solubility they can be applied during damp weather and even over a surface that is slightly damp.

Undercoats. When painting on raw wood, an undercoat is usually recommended. The undercoat serves as a sealer and forms a hard, tough coat for the next coat of paint. The disadvantage of using the same paint for the undercoat as the finished coat is that quite often spots are missed because there is no color separation for the eye to see what has been painted as the undercoat. Use a flat paint or shellac for the undercoat, as they will make it easier to see spots you missed. Open grain woods such as oak, walnut and ash have such large "pores" that even three or four coats of paint will not hide. These woods should always be sealed with an appropriate undercoat, regardless of whether the final finishing will be done with a latex paint or with an alkyd paint.

For interior work, there are three types of paints generally used: a flat finish for ceilings and walls; a semi-gloss or a full gloss for the woodwork in a room and a deck-type enamel if the floor is to be painted. The last mentioned, deck-type enamel, is a tough, varnish-based paint which can take floor traffic without undue wear.

Choosing Interior Paints

FOR SURFACES LISTED
BELOW USE PAINTS LISTED HERE

★ MEANS PRIMER OR SEALER
MIGHT BE NEEDED FIRST

	ASPHALT TILE FLOORS	CONCRETE FLOORS	DRY WALLS	HEATING DUCTS	KITCHEN AND BATH WALLS	LINOLEUM	METAL WINDOW FRAMES	NEW MASONRY WORK	OLD MASONRY WORK	PLASTER WALLS-CEILINGS	RADIATORS-HEAT PIPES	STAIRCASES-TREADS-RISERS	STEEL SURFACES-CABINETS	WALL BOARD	WINDOW SILLS-FRAMES	WOOD CASING-TRIM	WOOD PANELING	WOODEN FLOORING	VINYL-RUBBER-TILES
ALUMINUM PAINT				●			●		●		●								
CEMENT BASE PAINT								●	●									●	
CLEAR POLYURETHANE		●								●						●	●	●	
EPOXY PAINTS		●							●									●	
FLOOR VARNISH						●				●									★
FLOOR PAINT AND ENAMEL		●			●					●								●	
FLAT PAINT-ALKYD			★	★			★	★	●	★	★			★		★	★		
FLAT PAINT-LATEX			★					★	●	★				★					
GLOSS ENAMEL-ALKYD			★	★	★		★	★	●	★	★		★	●	★	★	★		
INTERIOR-VARNISH															●	●	●		
METAL PRIMER				●			●				●		●						
RUBBER BASE PAINT-NO LATEX		●		●	●		●	●	●	●	●	●	●	●	●	●	●		
STAIN		●								●						●	●	★	
SHELLAC			●		●					●						●	●	●	
SEMI-GLOSS-ALKYD			★	★	★		★	★	●	★	★		★	★		★	★		
SEMI-GLOSS-LATEX			★	★	★		★	★	●	★	●			★	★	★	★		
SEALER OR UNDERCOAT			●		●			●	●	●				●		●			
WOOD SEALER			●								●					●			
WAX-LIQUID OR PASTE		★				●										●	●	●	●
WAX-EMULSION	●	★				●												★	●

The flat paints come in latex or alkyd; semi-gloss in latex or alkyd; but the floor enamel is always an alkyd type. (There are latex paints made for floor use, but they will not wear as well as the alkyd types. The enamels or glossy paints will take more abuse, scrubbing, and washing than the flat-type paints.)

If in doubt as to which type of paint to use, consult the chart. Note that a star indicates that a primer or a sealer should be used before applying the finish coat, unless of course the surface has been previously painted and is in good shape.

After you have selected the proper paint, preparation is next in order. The right preparation consists of getting all of your paint supplies together (brushes, paints, thinners, dropcloths, ladders, rags, sandpaper, scraping tools, steel wool, rollers, pans, planks, hand tools, etc.) Then, if you are going to paint a room, remove all furniture, or else place it in the middle of the room adequately covered with drop cloths. Remove all light fixtures, or drop them from the ceiling; remove all outlet and switch plates; scrape away all loose paints, sand to a feather edge and apply a priming coat to freshly patched areas (use spackle for patching). Next, remove all hardware from doors, and windows; vacuum thoroughly to remove dust and debris; wipe all areas to be painted with a cloth dampened with water if you are going to use a latex paint and a cloth dampened with paint thinner if your paint will be in alkyd paint. Now you may start to paint!

And the place to begin, if you are planning to do a room, is the ceiling. Use white ceiling paint. This is a water-thinned latex paint that dries in an hour to a smooth, flat white and is practically odorless. The best way to paint a ceiling in order to avoid needless ladder shifting is to use 2 ladders and span them with a sturdy plank (two 3/4-inch lengths of plywood serve admirably). Mentally divide the ceiling into sections, say thirds the long way and thirds again the short way. Do one section at a time, using the plank as a walkway. You'll be pleasantly surprised at how much faster the work goes using the plank and ladder system instead of constantly shifting a single ladder.

When painting the ceiling, use as wide a brush as you can comfortably handle. Pros will generally use a 6-inch brush, but you may find this a bit too hard to manage, in which case a 4-inch brush will do the job nicely. Hairline cracks in the ceiling will be covered by the new paint. However, wider cracks should be filled with spackle or patching plaster. The last ceiling I painted had a fairly wide crack running the entire length of the ceiling. I applied spackling compound into the crack with my forefinger, waited until it was dry, sanded it smooth and painted the ceiling with perfect results. Wide cracks more than 1/8-inch in width, however, should be opened up with a beer can opener and then filled with spackle or plaster. Sand after drying, then paint.

If you are still in the same room, the next step is to paint the woodwork and trim. Use a semi-gloss enamel, either alkyd or latex type. If you are really fastidious, you will not only remove locks and hardware from the doors, but also the hinges and then paint the doors separately. Old paint can be removed from hinges by soaking the hinges in a lye solution; a tablespoon of lye to a quart of water makes a good paint remover. (*Caution:* Be careful working with lye; avoid spatters, and mix only in a glass or enamelware receptacle. *Never use an aluminum receptacle for mixing lye.*)

Let the hinges soak in the solution overnight, then remove them with tongs. Rinse them in cold water, let dry, and either spray them with clear lacquer or apply varnish to keep the bright finish of the hinges.

All trim (woodwork, doors, baseboards, molding, etc.) should be lightly sanded before painting and wiped clean before starting to paint. If your floors are carpeted wall-to-wall style, use a length of stiff cardboard to protect the carpeting from the brush as you paint the baseboards — and of course use drop cloths to protect all other areas of the room.

It is best to paint the trim of the room first and then the wall. Somehow it is easier — or maybe it just seems so — to paint the walls to a straight line adjacent to the trim, rather than the other way around.

Exterior Painting

If your house is more than two stories high, and cannot be reached with an extension ladder, my honest opinion is to forget it — not the painting, but the work. It would be best to get a professional to do the job. But if you can comfortably reach the top trim of your house with a ladder, there is no reason in the world why you cannot do an excellent exterior painting job. Remember, though, the preparation is just as important in exterior painting as it is in indoor work. Before you "prepare," you will need to have certain tools on hand. Here is a list:

- An extension ladder; remember that at least 3 feet of an extension ladder overlap each other, so bear that in mind if you are planning to buy one.
- Scraping tools such as sandpaper (coarse and medium), wire brush, a scraper, putty knife.
- Drop cloths — unless you don't mind changing the color scheme of some of your pet shrubs.
- Hammer and nails to nail down loose shingles and trim — use rust-resistant nails made of aluminum or galvanized nails.
- Caulking gun, caulking compound, putty.
- The paint — latex or alkyd, the choice is yours — plus its appropriate thinner, and of course brushes, rollers, and some rags to wipe up spills, your hands, and paint in the wrong places.

The best way to work is to follow the sun around the house. In other words, start at the side of the house that faces in an easterly direction, then go south, west, and finally north. When setting up the ladder at the selected site, extend it to the required height and secure the bottom of the ladder with a stake and a rope. The bottom of the ladder should be about 1/4 of its height from the wall. If the ladder happens to be in front of a door, either lock the door so it cannot be opened — with disastrous results to you, or put a sign on the door: "Open Slowly!" Otherwise you, like my neighbor, may be knocked off your ladder by a child tearing through the door in pursuit of a "cowboy."

Now that you have the ladder up, inspect the downspouts and gutters. Loose? Undoubtedly. Secure them with appropriate nails or spikes before proceeding. Loose caulking around the windows and doors? Of course. Pry out any loose or crumbling caulking. Brush out with a whisk broom and apply fresh caulking. Check the putty in the window, and if loose or crumbling, remove and replace.

Check shingles and clapboards. If loose, use aluminum or galvanized nails to secure them in place. Any cracks or nail holes should be filled with putty. A rust stain is an indication that a steel nail is disintegrating. Sand the area and apply shellac or a prime coat of paint to seal this spot from future deterioration. Sometimes a knot will bleed through paint, generally noticeable on clapboards. Sand the area and use shellac, not paint, to seal the knot from further bleeding.

Use the scraper, putty knife, or wire brush to remove all loose, flaking, and blistered paint. You will know when you get to the sound areas; if the paint stays "stuck," resisting your best efforts to remove it, proceed to the next blistered paint. You will know when you get to the sound areas. If the paint stays "stuck," resisting your best efforts to remove it, proceed to the next blistered area. When you get to a loose board, nail it in place; don't rely on your memory, thinking you will come back later to the nailing job — *do it now.* Cracks or holes should be filled with putty and given a coat of paint when dry. Use Naval Jelly® brand rust dissolver on any rusty iron or steelwork around the house. Apply a coat of red lead paint or metal primer to protect against further rusting. Any iron or steelwork around the house should be sanded and scraped if necessary and given a coat of red lead or metal primer to protect it from rusting.

If you are painting new work, three coats are suggested — primer and two finish coats. If the finish is in good condition on old work, a single coat will do the job. However, if a long time has elapsed between painting, then two coats are desirable. (*Caution:* Do not apply the second coat until the first coat has thoroughly dried, generally 24 hours for alkyd paints. A wrinkled finish is bound to occur if a second coat is applied too soon.)

How much paint will you need? A gallon of paint will cover about 500 square feet. Determine the average height of the house from the foundation to the eaves, and add 2 feet if the house has a pitched roof. Multiply this height by the distance around the foundation. This will give you the surface area in square feet. Divide this by 500 to get the number of gallons of paint you will need. Forget calculations about trim paint. The average house with 6 to 8 rooms requires only about a gallon of trim paint.

In addition to the paint and painting supplies mentioned before, you will need some old clothes. Wear hard-soled shoes instead of sneakers; you won't feel the rungs of the ladder through the soles. Set up the ladder to reach the highest part of the house and secure it as before. Please don't lean out from the ladder; your hips should always be between the rungs of the ladder. Use one hand on the ladder and the other one for the brush. (Industrial painters have a saying, "one hand for myself, one hand for the company.)

Choosing Exterior Paints

FOR ITEMS LISTED BELOW
USE PAINTS LISTED HERE

★ INDICATES PRIMER OR SEALER COAT MAY BE NEEDED

	ASBESTOS CEMENT	BRICK WORK	CONCRETE BLOCK	CONCRETE FLOORS	COPPER SURFACE	GALVANIZED METAL	IRON WORK	METAL WINDOWS	METAL ROOFING	METAL SIDING	NATURAL WOOD TRIM	STUCCO WORK	SHUTTERS AND TRIM	TAR FELT ROOF	WOOD SIDING	WOODEN WINDOW FRAMES	WOOD SHINGLES	WOOD FLOORING
ALUMINUM PAINT-EXT		●	●			★	★	★		★		●			●	●		
ASPHALT EMULSION												●						
CEMENT BASE PAINT		●	●									●						
EPOXY PAINTS				●														
EXTERIOR MASONRY LATEX	●	●	★									●						
EXTERIOR CLEAR FINISH											●							
HOUSE PAINT-LATEX	●	●	●			★	★	★	★	★	●	●	★		●	★		
HOUSE PAINT-OIL BASE	★	★	★			★	★	★	★	★		★	★		★	★		
LATEX TYPES	●	●	●	●		★	★	★	★	★	●	★			★	★		
METAL PRIMER						●	●	●	●	●								
PORCH AND DECK ENAMEL				●														●
PRIMER OR UNDERCOAT	●	●	●									●	●		●	●		
ROOF COAT-SURFACING														●				
ROOFING CEMENT														●				
SPAR VARNISH					●	●					●							
TRIM PAINT						★	★	★		★			★			★		
TRANSPARENT SEALER		●	●									●						
WATER REPELLENT PRESERVATIVE																	●	
WOOD STAIN											●						●	

Make an S-hook out of a wire coat hanger and use it to hang the can of paint. Suspend it so that is on the *outside* of the ladder, on the side of your painting hand. This way you can dip the brush into the paint can without having to reach awkwardly between your legs and jeopardizing your balance.

Chances are that the top of the house has some sort of trim that requires painting. Do it now or later — the choice is yours. If you want to do it now, you will have to supply yourself with a smaller can containing the trim paint, plus, of course, its own brush. And don't forget a rag dampened with the appropriate paint thinner, and a couple of pieces of sandpaper to feather out scraped areas, which you shouldn't have missed in the first place!

Caution: When painting the trim, make sure it is a *trim* paint, an outdoor enamel, not the paint used for the main part of the house. House paint has a special quality all its own — at least the good ones do — called *chalking*. This chalking prevents the paint from looking dirty due to weathering. Instead, a fine layer of paint is continually washed away by the rain to expose clean new paint. Of course, this can go on for a limited time before the wood beneath the paint is finally exposed — and then you will have to apply two coats of house paint instead of one.

Just how do you go about painting steps that must be used? Simple — paint every other step and when these are dry, paint the skipped steps. Or, you can paint just the right half or the left halves of the steps and finish the job the same way after that side has dried.

Railings around steps are painted last. Chip away all loose paint, sand thoroughly, or use Naval Jelly® . But, if your sanding, chipping, and wire-brushing has exposed the bare metal, use a metal primer before painting with exterior enamel. Pay special attention to the bottom of the railings. This is an area that even professional painters overlook, and it is the place where rusting starts. Believe it or not, you can even buy a brush with its handle at an angle so that you can paint this awkward area. And if you are really conscientious, you can check the bottom of the railing with a mirror!

Since there is more to a house than clapboards and trim, consult the chart for right paint to use on other parts of the house. A roller can be used to paint brick, stucco, and concrete. When using a roller, paint an edge first with a brush, then fill in with the roller.

Many front doors have a natural wood finish, protected by an exterior spar varnish to protect the door from weathering. If such is the case with your front door, sand it lightly, wipe clean with a rag dampened with paint thinner or turpentine and use varnish to finish the door. It is best to do this kind of work on a calm, warm day so no dirt or dust will adhere to the wet varnish.

Chapter 8

ROOF WORK

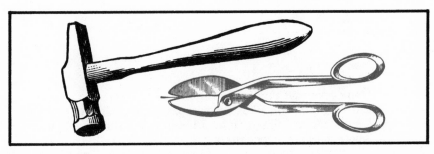

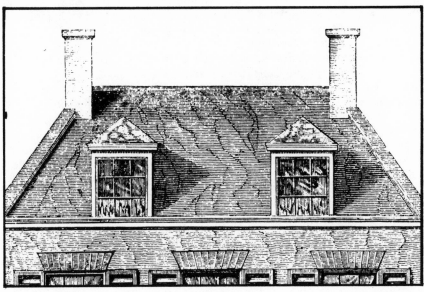

The first indication that a roof needs attention is a wet spot on the ceiling. Attend to a leaking roof without delay; disregarding a leaking roof means rot and decay in the supporting structure of the roof. The first step is to determine just where the water is penetrating from outside. The defective part of the roof is seldom directly over the wet spot on the ceiling. Water entering through a defect in the roof will usually take a meandering path, sometimes following a roof joist before dropping off to decorate the ceiling.

So, a bit of detective work is in order, and must be done during a rainstorm. Search the attic or crawl space under the roof with a powerful flashlight or a droplight. Start looking above the ceiling damage and try to determine where the water is coming from. Chances are you'll see a tiny rivulet meandering along the bottom of the roof boards and then dropping to the ceiling below. Follow the stream of water back to its beginning — like looking for the headwaters of the Nile!

When you have found the start of the leak, push or hammer a nail through the roof at this point. Don't worry about enlarging the hole; it is big enough already, and the extra nail hole will have little effect on the amount of water coming through the roof. On the next warm, sunny, windless day, the roof repair job should be started — and no excuse that it isn't raining and the roof isn't leaking.

Flat roofs are the easiest to repair. Their leaks generally develop along seams or around the base of a chimney or a vent pipe and in low spouts. If the roof is covered with gravel, sweep it away from the area to be repaired. Arm yourself with an old brush and a can of asphalt paint. Apply liberally around the base of the chimney, if that is where the leak has developed. After you are certain that the leak has been eliminated (wait for the next heavy rainstorm) you can sweep the gravel back into place.

How about blisters? They are common on many flat roofs. Cut through the middle of the blister with a sharp knife and force some roof cement (not the asphalt paint) under both sides of the cut. Then nail down the cut with wide-head galvanized nails. Apply another coat of roof cement to cover all the nailheads. Cut a patch of tar paper, slightly larger than the repaired area, and nail it over the repair job, with galvanized nails. Finish the job by coating this patch with the asphalt roof cement.

Large Repairs

If a fairly large section of the flat roof is in poor shape, it is best to cut out the damaged section. Apply a liberal coat of the roof cement to the exposed area and then nail down a patch of heavy tar paper or roofing felt over the cemented area. The patch should overlap the cut out area by at least 2-inches.

Next, make a second patch, larger by 2-inches all around than the first patch. Apply roof cement to the first patch, nail down the second patch over the first with galvanized nails and apply roof cement over this second patch, paying particular attention to the nail heads.

Asphalt Shingle Roof Repairs

Shingles are only installed on roofs that have a definite slope. They are never used on flat roofs. A sloping roof can be hazardous to work on unless certain precautions are taken. If the roof has an extreme slope, then a "chicken ladder" is called for. We don't know why they were given this name — possibly because they were first used in chicken houses for the chickens to roost on, or maybe just because you've got to be chicken to use them. At any rate, a chicken ladder is merely a light ladder made of 1 x 2s with a soft rubber backing on one side. The ladder is placed on the roof with rubber surface down, either tied so it won't slip or held at the bottom by an assistant. You can now walk on the rungs of the ladder; it will distribute your weight evenly — especially important when working on a slate roof. Of course, if the roof has a shallow slope, there's no need for the chicken ladder.

Now you are up on the roof and the nail you pounded in from the attic shows up at a torn shingle — the culprit. Lift up the shingle (carefully so it won't crack), and apply some roof cement liberally to the underside of the shingle. To make certain it will stay put, drive a couple of galvanized nails near the lower edge of the shingle, and most important, cover the nailheads with roof cement.

TAB ONLY

REPLACE SHINGLE

WOOD PROP

Shingle Replacement

Sometimes a shingle may be in such poor shape that the only respectable repair is to replace it. It's not too hard to do. Lift up the shingle above the damaged one. *Lift gently.* If the shingle is warm from the sun, it will not crack, which is why you should do roof repairs on a warm day. Remove the nails that hold the upper part of the damaged shingle in place. A pry bar, not a claw hammer, is best for this step.

Slip the new shingle in place under the lifted shingle. Nail down the new shingle while still holding up the upper shingle. Use galvanized roofing nails with broad heads. Apply roof cement to the nailheads and lower the upper shingle. If the upper shingle has a tendency to lift, apply a little cement to the underside of the upper shingle. This should do the trick.

Suppose you have no extra shingles on hand — what then? You can make the repair using a sheet of aluminum or copper. Cut the metal to the size of a shingle, cover it with roof cement and force it up under the upper shingle. Nailing will not be necessary as the light weight of the metal and the roof cement will hold it in place.

Valley Work

While you are up on the roof, take a good look at the valleys. These are V-shaped copper troughs between the sloped parts of the roof. Valleys tend to develop holes — and therefore leaks — at their lower ends. This is because they are subject to the wear of gravel, dirt, leaves and branches as this material is washed down by the rain. Such holes can be repaired with epoxy.

Sand the area to expose bright metal and then make up an epoxy mix. Apply the mixed epoxy *into* the hole and around the hole; smooth it out with a moistened finger. It will dry rock-hard overnight.

Flashing

The flashing around a chimney or a vent pipe is also subject to wear and leaks. See if the flashing has pulled away from the chimney. If it has, push it back and apply a generous layer of roof cement at the joint between the flashing and the chimney. A putty knife is a good tool for the application. Or try a mineral rubber in tape form, like Seal Patch.

Slate Roof Repairs

The one great advantage a slate roof has over a conventional asphalt shingle roof is its longevity. A slate roof will last for 50 years while as asphalt shingle roof is seldom guaranteed for more than 10 years by the installer.

But, slate roofs are much trickier to repair than an asphalt roof. Slate shingles, unlike asphalt shingles, cannot be pried up; they will snap and break. But slate shingles can be replaced. Here are four methods for replacing broken slate shingles which can be used by any homeowner:

1. The first step is to remove the damaged slate by pulling out the nails that hold the defective slate in place. This can be done rather easily by means of a simple tool you can make out of 1-inch strap iron. File two notches in it as shown in the drawing, and bend over the end for a hammering surface. To use it, slide it under the defective shingle until one of the notches engages one of the two nails that hold the shingle in place. Hammer on the bottom to remove the nail. Remove the second nail the same way.

Next, slide the new slate into position, making sure nothing is interfering with its placement, and mark off two spots for nails about halfway down in the exposed area. Remove the slate and punch two nail holes in it by the following method: Place the slate on soft ground, a gravel driveway, or a bed of sand. Place a nailset over each mark on the shingle and strike the nailset smartly with a hammer. The slate will not split. Reposition the slate on the roof and drive a couple of galvanized nails through these holes. Now cover up each nailhead with a dab of black asphalt roof cement.

2. This method calls for the use of a copper or aluminum strip to hold the slate in place. Remove the damaged slate as previously described and hammer in a couple of copper strips as shown in the drawing. Cover each nailhead with roof cement and slide the new slate shingle in place; make sure that you have at least a 2-inch overlap of copper strip. Now bend each copper strip over the edge of the slate and hammer it lightly to make it flush with the slate. The drawing illustrates this technique.

3. This method is used by many professional roofers. Remove the damaged slate with the tool described in the first method. Slide the new slate into position. (To ease the job you can apply some asphalt roof paint to the underside of the slate, if necessary.)

The next step is to drive a couple of copper or galvanized nails between adjacent slates *above* the new slate. This will hold the new slate in place and prevent it from shifting. To protect the nails from the weather — and leaks — you will have to cover the nailheads. Cut a strip of copper, about an inch wide and long enough to cover both nails. Gently pry up each adjacent slate (on each side of the nails) with a screwdriver. You don't have to pry too much, just enough so you can slip the copper strip between the slates far enough to cover the nails.

Keep the slates pried up by inserting wedges under their leading edges; a couple of spare screwdrivers will work fine. Push the copper strip with the aid of a screwdriver far enough so that both nails are covered, and remove the wedges. As an extra precaution, you can apply some roof cement over the copper strip.

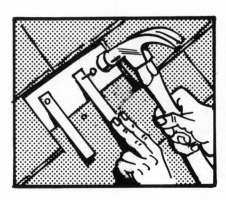

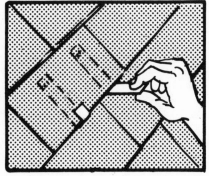

4. This method is probably the easiest of all to use. After removing the damaged slate and the nails with the tool described in the first method, slide the replacement slate into place, just to make sure there are no projections to hinder its final placement. Then remove the slate and mix up a batch of epoxy glue. Apply a generous dab at each corner of the bottom side of the slate, and at the two upper corners of the top side.

Now slide it into place; the epoxy will act as a lubricant. If necessary, tap the bottom of the slate with a block of wood to bring it into its proper place. The epoxy will have enough viscosity to keep the slate from sliding down as it cures. However, if the roof has a very steep pitch, use some masking tape to hold the slate in place; this will stop any possible movement. There's no need to remove the tape — it will disintegrate from exposure to the weather.

Chapter 9

HOW TO SAFEGUARD YOUR HOME

Actually, it is almost impossible to burglarproof a house, unless an armed guard is stationed outside for 24 hours a day. Even the United States Mint was once burglarized! Unfortunately (for the burglars) the room they broke into contained only pennies and they were captured, literally, by the trail they left.

However, you can make your home *burglar-resistant* to such an extent that any thief will take his business elsewhere. Here are sixteen practical ways to discourage a burglar from paying your home a visit. All of these ideas are in everyday use in a typical American town with the usual number of burglaries.

1. Warning Labels

A burglar would think twice — and maybe even three or four times — before trying to enter a home that has a warning label on the door to the effect that this particular house is protected by some sort of burglar-alarm system. How is he to know that the house is *not* wired? After all, it may be, even though the decal is just a "dummy" warning. You can get such decals from the companies that specialize in installing burglar alarm systems. Apply these decals on all doors, the back door as well as the front. These are excellent deterents, but if he also sees a large gong mounted over the front door, he is bound to be convinced.

2. Gongs

If our nefarious friend has had the courage to ignore the warning decal and has forced or picked the lock to the door and enters the house, he will be welcomed by an ear-splitting clanging from a gong mounted under the soffit of the house. The gong is actuated if an intruder takes just a single step beyond the front door. The secret is an 18 × 36-inch switch pad installed under a throw rug, welcome mat, or even under wall-to-wall carpeting. A step on the pad will automatically close a low voltage circuit that will cause the gong to sound — enough to frighten off any intruder.

Large hardware stores carry these pads, as well as the transformer and gong, for sale to retail stores to let the proprietor know when a customer has entered the store. To actuate the gong, just insert the plug into an AC outlet whenever you leave the house and no one is at home. Pull the plug when the family is at home.

3. Double Locks

Double lock your door, front as well as rear. A key-in-knob lock automatically locks the door when it is swung shut. Then a key must be inserted into a second lock to lock the door. This lock cannot be opened by hand, even if a burglar smashed the glass and reached behind to turn a knob, as the inside of the double lock can be operated *only by means of a key.* In other words, a key must be used to open or close the lock from the inside or outside.

Let's suppose a burglar has forced an entrance through the window, picks up a bulky television set, and tries to leave through the door. Sorry, Buster, the door cannot be opened without a key — even from the inside.

Always double lock your doors when you retire at night. However, keep an extra key near the double locked door (a nearby closet is a good spot) and make sure everyone in your family knows where this key is kept. This is important since you would want to get out of the house as quickly as possible in case of a fire or other emergency.

Incidentally, when you install a double lock, make sure that the key pattern is different from the first lock.

4. Protective Grills

If your front or rear door has a glass panel in it so that you can identify callers before opening the door, it should be covered with some sort of protective screen. The screen (it could be a decorative grill) will stop the burglar from smashing the glass and reaching through the hole to open the door. If you install the grill on the outside of the door, it is a good idea to use "one-way" screws to install the grill. These are screws that cannot be removed with ordinary screwdrivers.

5. Basement Windows

Basement windows are particularly vulnerable to entry. You can buy decorative grills that will fit any basement window. The grills come in two interlocking sections which are pulled apart to fit the width of the window. After a snug fit has been made, the two sections are locked in place with Allen bolts on the inside of the grill. Finish the installation with one-way screws inserted through the predrilled holes at each side of the grill. The screws engage the wood framework of the basement window.

6. Steel Bars

Another inexpensive way to protect basement windows of any size is by means of steel bars. Get several lengths of "soft" steel bars (easier to drill and cut than hard steel) 1/2-inch in cross section. and cut them with a hacksaw to the height of your basement windows. Next, drill a hole at each end of the bar for a one-way screw. Space the bars about 5 inches apart and drive the screws into the wood framework of the windows.

If you use conventional screws, file the heads down so that they cannot be unscrewed by an intruder or use epoxy to cover the head.

7. Patio Protection

Let's move to the inside of the house and see how we can protect it from burglary. That beautiful sliding glass patio door is especially vulnerable to entry. The lock can be forced, or a brick can be heaved through the glass so that the lock can be unlatched. The simplest way to prevent entry is to drop a length of wood into the track so that the door cannot be moved. Make sure the wood fits snugly so the door cannot be jiggled to force the lock. As a second safeguard, insert a length of wood in the *overhead* track. This length of wood should be slightly oversize so that it must be bowed and snapped into place.

8. Casements

Casement windows are comparatively simple to burglarproof. Close the window by turning the crank as tightly as possible, and then remove the crank. This way, if a burglar smashes a glass and reaches in to turn the crank, it will be impossible to open the window.

And for heaven's sake, don't leave the crank on the sill. Place it out of sight as well as out of reach.

9. Double-Hung Windows

Drill a hole through the inside sash and half way through the outside sash so that you can insert a nail through the window as shown. The nail should fit tightly in the hole so that jiggling the window up and down will not dislodge the nail.

The usual lock on double-hung windows, located where the two sashes meet in the middle, can sometimes be opened by an enterprising thief by inserting a knife between the sashes. Double-hung windows are prone to loseness at this area due to the wear caused by sliding the windows up and down. There are plenty of gadgets you can buy to safeguard double-hung windows, but the use of a nail is the simplest and most trustworthy.

10. Invisible Double Locks

These locks show no indication, from the outside of the door, that a second lock is safeguarding the entrance. So, if a thief smashes the window, slides back the bolt, and twists the door knob, he will still not be able to open the door.

Of course, let your family know where the keys to this lock are kept — again, a nearby closet is a good hiding place.

11. Hook And Eye

This is in the category of "why-didn't-I-think-of-this-before" ideas. It's just an ordinary hook and eye located at the top and bottom of a door and its frame. Garage and basement doors can be secured this way as the slight disfigurement of the hook and eye will not detract too much from the appearance of these utilitarian doors.

12. Screen Door Latch

It's simple, so why not do it! If you have a storm and screen door, you may as well utilize the latch provided on these doors. Always latch these doors when retiring for the night, and when you leave the house, latch all screen doors except of course for the one that lets you out of the house.

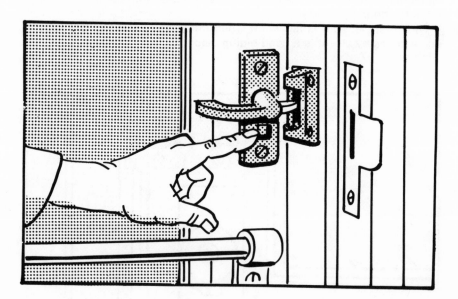

13. Clock-Operated Radio

Most people have some sort of a portable radio in the house. Get extra duty out of it by hooking it up to a clock timer that will turn on the radio at a predetermined time, say 6 o'clock to midnight. Tune the radio to one of those stations that have mostly talk shows or news reports, and set the volume at a conversational level so that a potential intruder will think there is someone in the house. Plug the timer into an outlet and set the timer controls to the afore-mentioned time interval. The kitchen is a good spot for this set-up since in most homes it is centrally located.

14. Clock-Operated Lights

There are many devices available to turn on lights in a house, but a few precautions should be observed. First of all, do not get the type with an electric eye that turns on the lights at dusk and off at dawn. This is too obvious a pattern, especially to a thief who is "casing" a house. Get the clock-operated timers so that you can select your own time interval for having the lights go on. Secondly, always insert a new bulb in the lamp. An old bulb is apt to burn out during your stay away from the house. A good idea is to use two bulbs by means of a two-way socket. This way if one bulb burns out, the other will still be doing the job. Thirdly, use a second timer and lamp in the bathroom to go on for a couple of hours after midnight. The only type of electric eye control that we do recommend is the kind that will turn on a lamp at dusk and turn it off at the time you want by means of a built-in clock.

15. Burglar Alarms

All of the previously mentioned protective devices are essential to a home's security, and will go far towards discouraging burglars. But an alarm system, which sounds a loud bell, horn or siren (when someone tries to break in), is being used more and more frequently. Although it may not prevent an entry by a determined professional burglar, it will frequently scare off vandals and spur-of-the-moment theives. The latter are responsible for a large percentage of residential break-ins.

Several companies now make low-cost alarm systems that can be easily installed, and are specifically designed for installation by do-it-yourselfers. They come with detailed instructions, and do not usually require inside-the-wall wiring. Home burglar alarms fall into two broad categories: space alarms that go off when an intruder passes a protected area or is inside the premises, and perimeter alarm systems that sound when a door or window is forced open.

16. Other Safeguards

A burglar will always be looking for telltale signs that you are away for an extended period of time — an unmown lawn, notes left for delivery people "to temporarily discontinue service", accumulations of daily newspapers and mail, plus the lengthy absence of cars in your driveway or garage.

Although notifying the milkman and other delivery people (well in advance) is your responsibility, the assistance of an alert, helpful neighbor is one of the most effective safeguards of all.

Chapter 10

CAR CARE

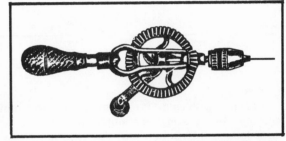

Locked Out

A car that won't start is a dilemma that every motorist faces at one time or another. One reason some motorists can't start their cars is because they have locked themselves out; the keys are coyly reposing in the ignition switch and all doors are locked.

You can guard against this mishap, which can be quite serious, by hiding a spare set of keys somewhere on the chassis that is readily accessible.

If you look under the fenders and bumpers of your car, you will notice many bolts that hold the car together. Wrap some tape around the keys (so dirt won't adhere to the "bit" part of the keys), enlarge the holes at the ends of the keys, if necessary, and mount the keys in one of the bolts. Use a wing nut to keep the keys in place. So, the next time you lock yourself out, unscrew the wing nut, remove the keys, strip off the tape — and you are all set.

Wrong Shift Position

Before you go on to more complicated procedures for starting a stalled car, check to be sure the shift lever is in *Neutral* or *Park*. No car will start if the lever is in any of the *Drive* positions or *Reverse*.

Out of Gas

Suppose the starter turns the engine over but still the engine won't fire. Is the fuel gauge showing gas in the tank? Even if it is, it may be empty — fuel guages can go haywire. Take the cap off the filler pipe and push the car up and down by tugging at the rear bumper. You should hear a sloshing noise. No matches, please.

Loose Battery Cables

Even if you have keys, the shift lever in the right position, and plenty of gas, sometimes the battery will not turn over the motor. The first thing to do then is to check the heavy cables to the battery. Loose cables will allow lights to go on and the horn to sound, but not enough current can pass to activate the starter motor.

Tighten the nuts that hold the cables in place. If you have no wrench, try pounding with a hammer, or even a heavy block of wood.

Corrosion

Rust can interfere with battery operation. This can be corrected by cleaning the battery posts with a wad of steel wool or with a battery cleaner. Spray the cleaner on the battery posts, let it soak in for three minutes and then wipe the posts clean with a damp cloth. Dry the posts and finish off the job properly by spraying a battery protector over the posts and cable ends.

Checking Spark Plugs and Distributor

Check the ignition for spark. Pull off one of the wires from a spark plug, wrap a handkerchief around it so you won't get a shock, and hold the end of the wire 1/4-inch from the tip of the spark plug (making sure the boot has been removed), or the engine block. Have someone crank the engine. You should see a spark jump from the wire to the plug or engine block. Nothing? Replace the wire and check the distributor. Remove the cap and see if it is cracked and check for a carbon deposit around the rim. Both of these are possibilities that will hinder starting.

Any carbon deposit can be wiped away, a cracked cap will have to be replaced. Check the wire to the coil — is it in place? Just to be on the safe side, push it in to assure good contact.

How about the wires leading to the plugs? If any are touching each other, the high voltage current may jump from one wire to another and bypass one or more plugs completely. Separate the wires (they should have a plastic bridge to keep them apart). Next, check the condenser and the connecting wires inside the distributor. Make sure they are all good and tight.

Dirty plugs make starting difficult. Use a plug cleaner, which is also good for cleaning the points on the distributor. After cleaning the plugs, gap them to the manufacturer's specifications. Wipe the porcelain with an oily rag before installing the boots.

Starting Fluid

Engine starting fluid is a highly volatile spray that frequently gets balky engines going. Two quick sprays into the carburetor throat after removing the air cleaner are enough. Replace the air cleaner before starting.

Dead Battery

Batteries go dead for a number of reasons. One of the most common causes is having left the lights on for an extended period of time while the engine is turned off. Exposure to cold, windy weather can be another cause.

Sometimes a battery fails because of insufficient charging, due either to lack of use or a slipping alternator belt. If you use your car infrequently, the battery will discharge by itself, and you will have to charge it every so often. But if your car is used nearly every day and the battery still runs down, check the belt that turns the alternator pulley. It should not have more than 1/2-inch of slack as you push it down at the midpoint with your finger.

Do not over-tighten the belt to prevent slipping; this will only put a severe strain on the pulley bearings. A better idea is to spray a Belt Grip dressing on the inside of the belt. This will help to prevent the belt from slipping around the alternator pulley. A slipping belt does not turn the alternator fast enough to generate the current required to keep the battery up to par.

If a battery is four or five years old, and/or is unable to hold a charge, the only solution is to get a new one.

The belt driving the alternator, the fan, and sometimes other parts of the car can be tightened or loosened by loosening the bolts that hold the alternator to the engine block. These are generally the two bolts that pass through a flange on the alternator body and are secured by nuts.

If your engine is clean, you should have no trouble locating them. Loosen the two nuts so that the alternator can be swung, either toward the belt to tighten it, or away from the belt for loosening.

If you have trouble loosening these nuts, which is a possibility as they are exposed to road salts and tend to corrode, spray the nuts with a penetrating lubricant; it does a quick and easy job of freeing frozen nuts and fittings. Spray it on the affected parts, wait a few minutes to allow the solvent to penetrate and do its job, then apply a wrench and some muscle power to the frozen nuts. You should be able to back them off. Now adjust the alternator so that the belt has 1/2-inch of slack. *NOTE:* Defective voltage regulators can cause dead batteries.

Push-starting a Car

If your car has a manual transmission you can get it started with a push from another car. First make sure the bumpers will not interlock. Tell the friendly driver of the pushing car not to exceed 10 miles per hour. Turn the key to *On* — not to the *Start* position — and put the car into second or high gear. Step on the clutch, and as your car picks up speed, engage the clutch slowly. Your car should now start. Accelerate away from the pushing car to let the driver know the car is started. But before making any big travel plans, have your battery charged, or replaced if necessary.

Cars with automatic transmissions cannot be started by pushing until a speed of at least 25 miles per hour is achieved, and some can't be started at all by pushing.

Jump-starting a Car

To safely jump-start cars with automatic transmissions, you need jumper cables and a car with a good battery. Leave the good car running and park it so both its battery and the dead battery are near each other. This may mean facing both cars together, or parking them next to each other.

The following six steps show the safe way to jump start your car:

1. Attach the clamp on the battery cable to the positive (+) terminal of the good battery.

2. Attach the other end of the cable to the positive (+) terminal of the dead battery (make sure both are positive terminals).

3. Shielding your eyes with your hand, attach one end of the other cable to the negative (–) terminal of the good battery.

4. Attach the other end of the cable (attached to the negative terminal of the good battery) to the engine block (the "ground") of the car with the dead battery.

5. After car battery has been jumped, and the car is running, wait until it runs smoothly before disconnecting cables (this protects delicate electronic equipment).

6. Proceed to disconnect the cables in the exact opposite order from which they are attached.

Be careful. Batteries contain sulfuric acid and generate explosive gases during this type of operation. Spark or flame could ignite these gases and possibly cause an explosion. So make sure you do not smoke while jump-starting a car. Also, avoid touching cables together while they are connected, as this can cause sparks.

Preventive Measures

Of course, anticipating trouble, and taking steps to prevent it, is your best insurance. During the winter this is especially important. The cold weather lowers the starting power of the battery, and also tends to congeal the oil in the crankcase — a combination that may spell disaster in the morning.

Hydrometer and Battery Charger

An investment in a hydrometer and a battery charger is good insurance. Check all six cells in the battery. If the hydrometer indicates half-charge or less, put the battery on charge overnight. Don't worry about over-charging the battery. Modern chargers taper off their charging rates as the battery is brought up to full charge.

Crankcase Heater

Another device to help the car get started in the winter is a crankcase heater. This is just a long electrically heated rod that is pushed into the crankcase after removing the dipstick. It uses very little current, but keeps the oil in the crankcase warm and fluid so that there is less drain on the battery when starting.

Light Bulb

Still another idea is to place a lighted 100-watt bulb in the engine compartment. This will keep both the engine and the battery warm, thus expediting starting. (In Alaska they have hitching posts for automobiles with an electrical outlet for this very purpose.)

A Clean Ignition System

The high voltage used in the ignition system is very susceptible to moisture and the slightest trace of moisture in the system will affect ignition. Dirt on wires and the coil tend to trap moisture, adversely affecting the efficiency of the ignition system, and making it hard to start the car.

Keep the engine clean. Wipe off all wires, the coil, and the spark plug boots with a cloth. When they are free of dirt, spray all the ignition components with an ignition sealer to protect the parts against moisture. If the spark plug wires are wet, give each one an extra spraying. Wait a few minutes to give the spray a chance to work and then start the engine.

You may want to use a grease-cutting cleaner such as an engine degreaser. You hold the spray can about a foot from the engine and associated parts, and spray liberally. Let it soak in for 15 minutes to do its work (it won't affect wires or the distributor), then hose off the loosened dirt and grime with water. This product can be used to clean the garage floor as well. Spray it over the grease spots on the floor, wait 15 minutes, then flush away with a garden hose.

A clean engine always starts more readily than a dirty one. And that also applies to PCV (Positive Crankcase Ventilation) valves, automatic chokes, the carburetor and the manifold heater. Use a carburetor and parts cleaner to clean these areas. It comes with a convenient tube that is fitted into the spray head to reach less accessible places. Use this product when the engine is cold for best results.

Oil Changing

Car makers compete with each other in telling motorists how infrequently the oil needs to be changed in their respective cars. (At one time all manufacturers recommended an oil change every 1,000 miles.) But regardless of the mileage or time interval you use in changing oil in the crankcase, the oil in your car should be drained only when it is *hot.*

If you leave your car at a service station or a dealer for an oil change, he will do the job at his convenience, most likely after the car has been standing for a few hours. But if you drain the oil after coming home from a long trip, then the oil in the crankcase is hot and rather thin, and that is the time to do the job. Place a pan under the crankcase and use an open-end or socket wrench to remove the crankcase plug. Let the oil drain overnight. This way you will be assured that every drop of old oil has been drained from the car. The next day, install a new oil filter, replace the crankcase plug, and add the required amount of oil Another option is to use a 5 minute motor flush to clean the engine and remove all old sludge and dirt.

Dots, Dimples, Dents, and Other Disfigurements

So your pride and joy has received a few nicks in the parking lot or part of the body beautiful has rusted. No need to dispose of your sweetheart.

Those small eye-catching dimples that all cars harvest in parking fields can be easily eliminated with touch-up enamel. These enamels are available in colors to match all American cars and some European cars in auto accessory shops. To get rid of these spots, first clean off all dirt and wax from the affected areas using a rag or cloth dampened with paint thinner. Wipe the areas dry and apply the touch-up paint just as it comes from the bottle or tube.

After a few weeks have elapsed, it will be safe to polish that area, and in time, sun and rain will weather the touched up spots so it will hardly be distinguishable from the original paint job. Of course by that time, the car will undoubtedly have a few more places to touch up. Well, that's how it goes. But you will be pleasantly surprised by the difference touching up those spots does make to the appearance of the car.

Deep Scratches

But how about deep scratches and dents in the car? It's no particular problem to solve; just a bit more time is involved, and a few more items will be needed.

Use paint thinner, not gasoline — to remove all wax and dirt from the deep scratch or dent. (If the area is very rusty, use Naval Jelly to clean out and remove the rust.) Wipe clean and sand the area thoroughly with a medium grit sandpaper followed by a fine grade of sandpaper.

Next, fill in the depression with spot putty. Don't try to fill in the entire area with a single application if the dent is deep. Instead, apply the putty in layers, each one not more than 1/8-inch thick. After the putty has dried, sand it thoroughly and carefully to the level of the surrounding area. Clean with a tack cloth to make sure all dust and dirt have been removed.

Now mark off the surrounding area with tape and spray sandable primer sealer over the repaired spot. After the primer is completely dry, use fine sandpaper and water to smooth out the repair job. Any possible pinholes should be filled at this time with spot putty. After the putty has dried, and again using fine sandpaper and water, apply two more coats of primer.

Continue using the sandpaper and water treatment until you are completely satisfied that the job is as smooth and as perfect as your conscience will allow. Clean the area thoroughly with a tack cloth and spray on a couple of coats of paint to match the rest of the car. Wait at least three days before using a rubbing compound. The compound will bring a lustrous glow to the repaired area, which will actually look even better than the rest of the car.

If at all possible, try to push out the dent from the inside of the car. It will still need some filling, but possibly not quite as much. But regardless of whether the dent has been pushed out or not, sand the area to the bare metal. A power sander is handy for this step. Make sure all rust is gone; rust that is still lodging in crevices can be removed with Naval Jelly.

Next roughen the area with coarse sandpaper and clean with a tack cloth. There should be no dust, dirt, or grease in the cavity at this point. Auto body solder is a body filler that is extremely easy to use. Ladle out the filler with a plastic spreader, applying it in layers not more than 1/8-inch thick at a time, with a four hour drying period between each layer. Keep this up until the dent has been filled up to the surrounding area.

This process need not immobilize your car. You can drive around while allowing the body solder to dry. If you have built up the dent, and it now resembles a small hill, sand it down with a flexible sander of the kind shown in the drawing. Clean the area with a tackcloth, mask the surrounding area to guard against overspray, and spray on a coat of sandable primer sealer. Careful — do not allow the primer to run, drip, or sag. Sand, wipe, and apply another coat of primer. Repeat this routine at least two more times.

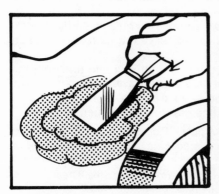 

After the primer has dried, it will be safe to sand the repair with fine sandpaper and water. Keep adding water during the sanding operation; this assures a superfine finish. Any pinholes at this time can be filled in with spot putty. Wait a few hours to allow the putty to dry, and sand again with fine sandpaper and water. Clean thoroughly and apply two more coats of the primer.

The "look" of the primer will determine the appearance of the final paint job so do a good careful job at this point. Sand the primed area with an extra-fine waterproof sandpaper and water. After the area is dry (you can hasten the drying by wiping with a clean cloth), a finish coat of paint or enamel can be sprayed on.

When spraying, move the gun or can so that it will always be the same distance from the repair. *Don't spray in an arc.* If you do, the center will be getting more paint than the sides. Apply at least three coats of paint or lacquer, spraying on the next coat as soon as the first coat is dry to the touch. If a run develops, leave it alone. Wait until it has dried, then sand it off. After three days it will be safe to use a rubbing compound on the paint job. This should restore your car to showroom condition.

Big Dents

These are the kind that bring tears to the eyes — especially if it is either a fairly new car or a classic vintage car. Don't cry; you can fix it yourself, and it's not too hard. First, pull out the dent as much as possible. This can be done with a commercial dent puller as shown in the drawing, or you can improvise one yourself as follows: Insert a self-tapping screw into the low part of the dent, span the dent with a block of wood and use a claw hammer to pull on the screw, making sure the heel of the claw hammer is resting on the wood.

Once the dent has been pulled out as much as the sheet metal has allowed you are ready for the next step. Remove all paint and rust around the dent and as much as possible inside the dent. An electric drill with a sandpaper disc attachment makes short work of this step. Now for the interesting part......

Get a container of Black Knight™ (or White Knight™ if the car is a light color) Auto Body Repair Kit and mix the hardener with the body filler. The correct proportions are 1/4 teaspoon of the cream hardener to about 3 tablespoons of the body filler; mix thoroughly until it is a uniform dark gray.

Now ladle the mixture into the dent, using a putty knife or plastic spreader. Make sure the mix is in good contact with the bottom of the dent. If the dent is large and rather deep, it is a good idea to drill a number of 1/8-inch holes at random so the filler material will have an extra good purchase. Fill the dent so that it is slightly above the surface of the surrounding metal. Let it dry; it will only take about 10 minutes and sanding can take place after a 30 minute wait. Use sandpaper, medium or coarse, to shape the dried filler to the contour of the body or fender. Finish sanding with fine sandpaper as shown in the drawing.

Next, clean the area with the tackcloth to remove all dust. Mask the surrounding area with tape, about 2 or 3 inches beyond the repair area. Spray sandable primer sealer over the repair area, being careful not to spray beyond the masking tape.

Rust-Outs

These problems are caused by generous use of chemicals and salt for road clearing during snowstorms. It's good for the salt and chemical companies, but it sure puts a dent in the motorists' pocketbooks.

The best way to protect your car from the ravages of winter is to rustproof it. There are professional rustproofing shops all over the country that do just this, but you can save money by doing it yourself.

The Auto Rust Proofing Kit has everything you need to do the job, and easy-to-follow instructions. Three of the aerosol cans contain a special formula for the car's inner cavities and two have a different formula to protect exterior portions including the bottom. Plastic extension tubes (for spraying into the inner cavities), spraying heads and plastic plugs are also included.

If you didn't have the foresight to rustproof your car and the inevitable rusting has now occurred, fear not; this problem can be licked. Lightly pound the rusted areas to see just how much of it still has some good metal behind it. Use a chisel and a hammer to bend back all the rotted metal. You can tell when you have gotten to the "good" metal as it will be tough to bend back. Sand a section all around this rusted area: 2 or 3 inches around the rust should be sufficient. Naval Jelly will do a quick and efficient job of removing rust. The surface to be repaired should be clean, and free of rust or paint.

This repair can be done with the help of a Fiberglass Repair Kit. The kit contains everything needed to make a perfect repair on any rusted-out metal.

Measure the area to be repaired and cut a piece of fiberglass an inch larger all around than the repair area.

Pour the resin into the mixing tray and add the hardener in the following proportion: 30 drops of hardener to 4 ounces of resin. After mixing, the solution should be used within 30 minutes as it will start to "set" as soon as the hardener is added to the resin. Now dip the previously cut piece of fiberglass into the tray, making sure it is thoroughly immersed. Remove the cloth, let it drain for a second or two, and place it over the prepared area. Stretch out all sides to make sure it is good and tight. Any areas that appear uneven or dry should be treated to more of the mix; just apply it with a spoon or flat stick.

Sit back and relax. Allow the patch to dry for about 30 minutes, at which time it will be hard and ready for sanding or filing. Sand the entire area with fine sandpaper. If any low spots appear, they can be filled in with spot putty. Allow the putty to dry, and sand the area again. Then wipe with a tack cloth to remove the dust. Now, mask the surrounding area with masking tape and newspapers to prevent overspray.

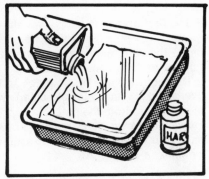
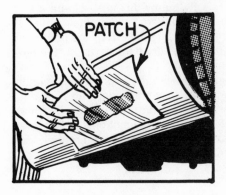

Spray on a coat of sandable primer sealer in the desired color. After the primer is dry, sand again with a fine waterproof sandpaper. Keep adding water as you do the sanding. If necessary, spray on an additional coat of the primer, but remember, sanding again will be necessary.

If any pinholes appear, they can be filled in with the spot putty and again sanded after the putty has dried (usually 3 to 4 hours).

The next step is to spray the primed area with lacquer or paint. Use a tack cloth to remove all dust before starting to spray. Keep the spray gun or can at a constant distance from the job — about 12 inches away. Shake the can for at least 3 minutes to assure complete mixing of the color. After a few days have elapsed it will be safe to use a rubbing compound to blend the repaired area to the surrounding area of the car. After a few weeks of exposure to sun and weather, the repaired area will be indistinguishable from the rest of the car.

Repairing Surface Rusting

Small, rusted out areas can be repaired rather easily with a new product called Ultra Patch® fiberglass repair material. The unusual feature of this material is that it dries rock-hard by exposure to sunlight or even a sun lamp!

The first step is to sand away the rusted or damaged surface to the bare metal. Then pound the area lightly with a hammer to depress it slightly below the surrounding area of the car, so that the finished repair job will be flush with the adjacent metal.

Next, cut a piece of the patch to the required size, allowing for a 1-inch overlap. Use a tack cloth to clean away all the dust and dirt. Strip away the blue backing from the patch and apply it to the area to be repaired, with the sticky side down. Make sure it is pressed down firmly; run the palm of your hand over the entire surface to assure good contact. *Make sure there are no wrinkles in the patch.*

The next step is the easiest part of the repair. Just allow the sun to do the job! In bright sunshine and at a temperature of 75°, the patch will harden, ready for sanding, in about 1 hour; a partly sunny day may require 4 or 5 hours. But if the sun refuses to cooperate, a sunlamp will do the job just as well — even faster. Place the sunlamp about 8 inches from the patch and keep it on for about 20 minutes. The patch will dry hard, ready for the next step — removing the clear plastic film.

Use a medium grade sandpaper and sand from the edges to the middle; this will "feather" the edges of the patch. After sanding, wipe away all dust and spray on a coat of sandable primer sealer. Let it dry and sand with waterproof sandpaper; use water while sanding. Any visible pinholes can be filled in with spot putty. Allow the putty to dry before sanding, then apply two more coats of the primer, sanding thoroughly between coats.

The last step, of course, is to apply the paint or lacquer of your choice. Spray evenly and apply at least two coats. The second or third coat can be applied as soon as the preceding coat has dried to the touch. After three to four days, it will be safe to finish off the job with a rubbing compound and waxing.

Muffler Work

There was a time when the muffler lasted for the life of the car. Those days are gone. Road salts and the light gauge metal used for mufflers and tailpipes mean frequent replacement, or repair to give them a new lease on life. These parts can be repaired with repair kits on the market. Muffler and tailpipe bandage is exactly what its name implies — first aid for the ailing muffler.

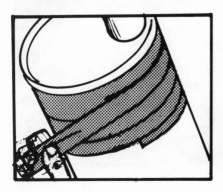

To use, the area around the hole in the muffler is scraped clean with coarse sandpaper, steel wool, or a wire brush. Then drive the car to warm up the muffler. Next, the protective backing on the bandage is peeled off and the bandage wrapped around the muffler. Make sure the bandage has a generous overlap of at least 1-inch. Each side of the bandage should be secured with masking tape or light wire to keep it in place while the epoxy in the bandage cures. Curing is affected by heat as the car is driven. A 30-minute drive is enough to "set" the epoxy into a permanent bond with the muffler. The bandage can also be used to seal leaks in the tailpipe.

Installing a New Muffler

When installing a new muffler, make sure that the joints between the muffler and the tailpipe and the muffler and the exhaust manifold are sealed. Gases escaping from these two points can be a lethal hazard. If you are planning to do your own muffler installation (a common Saturday chore for many Americans) apply some muffler and tailpipe sealer to these areas. Apply it in a 1/4-inch layer around the inside of the larger pipe, then make the installation. This product can also be used to seal small holes in an old muffler, and doing this will prevent them from getting bigger and possibly save you the cost of a new muffler.

If you are having trouble removing that old muffler, due to the rust on the nuts and fittings, squirt some penetrating lubricant over the affected parts. Wait a few minutes and then apply the wrench. It's bound to work, just be patient.

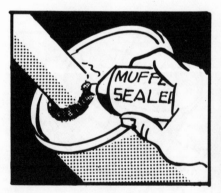

Appliance Touch-Up Specially formulated glaze for touching up nicks and scratches on porcelain and enamel surfaces. Will not crack, chip, peel or yellow.

Auto Rust Proofing Kit is the inexpensive do-it-yourself way to prevent your car from rusting out. Contents include special formulas for parts of car which are prone to rust.

Battery Cleaner Spray it on — in 3 minutes wash corrosion off.

Battery Protector Stops terminal corrosion — increases battery life. Spray on battery terminals, in or out of storage.

Belt Grip Excellent dressing that stops V-belts and fan belts from squeaking and slipping.

Black Knight™ or White Knight™ Auto Body Repair Kit Flexible, fast-drying polyester auto body filler repairs dents and holes in car bodies. Kit contains filler, cream hardener, applicator and fiberglass screening for bridging over rusted-out areas.

Cam Kleen® * Liquid cleaner or aerosol for removing mineral deposits, grime, rust spots from ceramic tile, grout, brick, slate and concrete.

Cam Kote® * Specially formulated aerosol that seals out dirt and grime while it polishes and protects tile, grouting, slate and marble surfaces. Use after cleaning with Cam-Kleen for best results.

---

* *A registered brand of Woodhill Permatex.*

Carburetor & Choke Cleaner Dissolves dirt, lead, gum and carbon deposits from carburetors, automatic chokes and PCV valves. Will not harm catalytic converters.

Contact Cement For all repairs and projects that cannot be clamped. Bonds on contact for a permanent water-resistant bond. Withstands temperatures up to 215°F.

Darn® * all purpose fabric mender — for use on all wool, cotton, leather, canvas and synthetic material. Withstands washing, ironing and boiling. Safe and non-flammable.

Engine D-Greaser Cleans dirty, oil-coated engines. Cuts through oil, grease, dirt and grime. For all engines, lawnmowers, garage floors and similar areas.

E-Pox-E® * Appliance Enamel Sprays a high-gloss, porcelain-like finish on appliances, tiles and bathroom fixtures. Adheres to metal, porcelain, wood, concrete and glazed surfaces.

E-Pox-E® * Cement and Filler Bonds, seals and fills holes and cracks in metal, concrete, wood, fiberglass, brick and ceramics. When dry, can be drilled, tapped, sanded, molded and painted. Waterproof.

E-Pox-E® * Fiberglass Repair Kit Complete kit for bridging over holes, rotted and rusted out areas in fiberglass, glass, wood and metal.

E-Pox-E® * Glue Strongest glue which dries to a clear and permanent bond. Bonds and repairs plastic, wood, metal, glass, ceramics — almost anything to everything.

E-Pox-E® * Ribbon An epoxy which works like putty, by kneading two ribbons together and applying to almost any surface. It will not sag, drip or run. Use it to seal plumbing leaks, patch masonry, bond outdoor lights, fix stripped screw holes...and for many other jobs that require super chemical resistance. It is moldable, sculptable, sandable and fits a wide variety of applications.

Fixture Adhesive Use where nails screws and ordinary glue won't work. Does not become brittle. Shock, water, temperature and acid-resistant. Safe, non-flammable, contains no toxic fumes.

Flexible Sander Conforms to the shape of the surface being sanded.

Furniture Tough-Up Kit Complete kit for filling holes, repairing nicks and scratches and hiding blemishes on all wood finishes. Kit contains Matchwood plastic woodfiller and four matchstick stain crayons.

Household Cement Ready-to-use, all purpose household cement. Adheres to wood, glass, china, metal, leather, etc. Dries to a clear, permanent bond.

Liquid Solder Non-metallic. Apply cold — without use of tools, heat or flame — adheres to almost any surface. Ideal for repairing plumbing leaks, seams in metal pails, gutters and downspouts.

Liquid Steel Ready-to-use as a filler or adhesive. Seals, fills and repairs almost any metal surface. Once dry, can be filed, drilled and sanded. Can be painted over.

Lock-It™ Anaerobic liquid lockwasher — stops nuts, bolts and screws from loosening. Vibration will not undo it. Secures parts on bicycles, lawnmowers, cars, tools and thousands of other items.

* *A registered brand of Woodhill Permatex.*

Muffler & Tailpipe Bandage E-Pox-E® * impregnated wrap-around bandage. Chemically welds around muffler. Permanently repairs holes and leaks in all types of exhaust systems — seals out poisonous fumes. Withstands heat up to 500°F.

Naval Jelly® * brand rust dissolver chemically removes rust from metal surfaces.

Penetrating Lubricant Frees frozen nuts and bolts — oils, cleans, preserves and protects in one application. Great for sticky windows, locks and doors.

Pizazz® * vinyl and rubber dressing and protectant especially recommended to rejuvenate anything made of vinyl, plastic, rubber or leather.

Safe Contact Cement Water-based contact cement. Non-flammable and non-sniffable — contains no toxic fumes. Bonds on contact for repairs that can't be clamped.

Seal Patch™ weather-resistant rubber in a ready-to-use tape form. Instantly stops all types of leaks. Adheres to all metal, glass, plastic and porous surfaces.

Solvo Rust® * super penetrant, lubricant and rust dissolver.

Super Glue-3® * cyanoacrylate, one-drop, bonds in seconds glue. For bonding all non-porous material — jewelry, china, glassware, bumper strips, loose knobs and hundreds of other items. Dries to a clear and permanent bond.

Tub'n Sink Jelly™ Chemically dissolves lime, rust and hard water discolorations from porcelain, fiberglass and acrylic surfaces.

Tub'n Tile Sealer with silicone Caulk to use on tiles, plaster and around tubs, sinks and wash basins. Acrylic-resin based, non-toxic and non-flammable. Waterproof, stays white and is mildew-resistant.

Ultra Patch® * fiberglass repair material. Ready to apply, it hardens when exposed to sunlight or sunlamp and forms a strong, permanent, waterproof repair.

Formula V vinyl adhesive clear formula. Repairs rips, tears and burns in vinyl and leather articles. Ready to use. Dries to a clear, flexible bond. Ideal for use on auto upholstery, luggage, handbags, furniture and toys.

* A registered brand of Woodhill Permatex.

INDEX

A

Abrasives, 22-23
Adhesives, types of, 16-22
Alarm, burglar, 121
Alkyd-base paint, 42
Appliances, refinishing of, 60
Asphalt shingles, 107
Automobile (See Car)
Awl, 11

B

Backsaw, 9
Bathtub, sealing leaks, 50
Battery, car
   cables, 125
   charger, 127
   dead, 125-126
Bolts, 15
Box joints, 26
Brushes, paint, 100

C

C Clamp, 30, 37
Cabinet screwdriver, 9
Car, 123-136
   dents in, 129-131
   jump-starting of, 126-127
   push-starting of, 126
   rust-proofing of, 132-134
Carpet (See Rug)
Casements, 118
Caulk, 50, 102
Ceiling
   lowering of, 38-39
   panels for, 40-41
   painting of, 100
Cellulose adhesives, 21
Cement paint, 37-38
Cements, 17-18
Ceramic tile, 49-50
Chair rungs, tightening, 80
Chalking, 104

Chips
  in enamel, 60
  in glassware, 58-59
  in porcelain, 49, 60
Chisels, 11
Chlorinated rubber paint, 42
Claw hammer, 8
Contact cement, 17-18
Coped joints, 28
Copper pipes, 51
Cord, electric, 85
Corrosion, 125
Countertops, 63-64
Crankcase heater, 127
Crosscut saw, 9
Cross-over joints, 27

D

Dado joints, 26
Dampness, basement, 35
Dents, car, 129-131
Dishes mending of, 58-59
Distributor, car, 125
Doors
  hitting pipe, 34
  burglar-proofing of, 113-116, 118-120
  sticking, 78-79
Dovetail joints, 26
Drawers, sticking, 77
Drop cloths, 101
Drills, 11
Dripping faucet, 67-71

E

Edge-to-edge joints, 27
Efflorescence, 42
Enamel surfaces, 60-61
Epoxies, 16-17, 47, 49, 58
Extension cord, 85
Extension ladder, 101

F

Fasteners, 12-15
Faucets
  bathroom, 51
  replacement of washer in, 73
  types of, 67-71
  washerless, 74
Flaking paint, 102
Flashing, 109
Floors
  painting concrete, 42
  squeaks in wood, 81-82
  replacing tile, 62
Furniture
  repairing vinyl tears, 66
  fixing scratches, 76

G

Gaskets, 66
Glassware, mending of, 58-59
Glues
  animal, 19
  hot melt, 21
  water-resistant, 20
  waterproof, 20
  wood, 21
  white, 16
Gong, entry, 115
Grading, 35
Grill, door, 116
Groundwire, 86-87
Grout, 50

H

Hacksaw, 8
Hammers, 8, 48
Hook and eye, 120
Hot melt glue, 21
Hydrometer, 127

I

Ignition, car, 128

J

Jeweler's screwdriver, 9
Joints, uses of, 26-28
Joists, 38, 82
Junction box, 52-53

L

Lamp, parts of, 84-85
Lap joints, 26
Latch, screen door, 120
Latex paints, 42, 98
Leaks
  in bathtub, 50
  in ceiling, 106
  in faucet, 74
  in pipe, 36-37
Levels, 11
Light bulb, 127
Lights, clock-operated, 121
Locks
  double, 115, 119
  screen door, 120
  window, 119-120

M

Mastics, 20
Measuring devices, 10
Mending fabric, 32
Miter box
  construction of, 28-29
  uses of, 11
Miter joints, 27
Mortised joints, 26
Muffler, car, 135-136

N

Nails, 12

O

Oil, car, 128
Outlet, electric
  defective, 86
  installation of, 52-54

P

Paint, exterior
  how to choose, 103-104
  preparing for job, 101-102
  safety on job, 102-103
Paint, interior
  how to choose, 98-99
  preparing for job, 100
Panels, 40-41, 92-93
  adhesives for, 93
Pastes, 19
Phillips screwdriver, 9
Pipes, leaks in, 36-37
Planes, 9
Pliers, 10
Porcelain
  repair of, 49, 60
  removing stains from, 51

R

Radio, clock-operated, 121
Ratchet screwdriver, 9
Refrigerator, 66
Ripping hammer, 8
Right-angle screwdriver, 9
Roofs, 106-112
  flat, 106-107
  flashing on, 109
  slate, 110-112
Rugs
  securing, 89-90
  prevention of raveling, 90
Rustproofing
  car, 132-134
  railings, 104

S

Safety
  on ladder, 102-104
  with electricity, 86
Sandpaper, types of, 22-23
Saws, hand, 9
Screwdirvers, 9
Screws, 13-15
Shaver outlet, 52
Shower handles, repairing, 48

Shingles, roof
  repair of, 107-108
  replacement of, 109-112
Silicone sealants, 20
Sills, window, 64-65
Sink
  chips, 49
  stains, 51
Slates, roof, 110-112
Sledge hammer, 8
Soap dish, 48
Socket, electric, 84
Spark plugs, 125
Spiral Screwdriver, 9
Splices, 23
Squares, 10
Steel bars, 117
Steel tape, 10
"Stubby" screwdriver, 9
Surform, 9
Switches, electrical
  wall, 87
  replacement of, 88
  three-way, 89

T

Three-way joints, 27
Tiles, ceiling, 39
Tiles, floor
  ceramic, 49-50
  replacement of, 61-62
Toilet bowl, stains, 51
Toilet tank
  adjustment and repairs, 54-56
  condensation, 56
Tools, 8-12 (See also specific items)
Trim paint, 104

U

Undercoats, 98

V

Valley work, 109

W

Wall, switches, 87-89
Wall, exterior
  painting of, 101-104
Wall, interior
  installing panels on, 92-93, 95
  papering of, 95-97
  painting of, 37-38, 98-100
Wallpaper
  adhesives for, 21
  hanging of, 96-97
  preparation of surface for, 96
  removal of, 95
Washer, faucet, 73
Water, basement, 35-36
Water hammer, 43-44
Water-resistant glue, 20
Waterproof glue, 20
White glue, 16
Windows
  protection
    basement, 117
    double-hung, 119
    locks for, 11, 119-120
    patio, 118
  new sill for, 64-65
Wire nuts, 86
Wiring, for outlet, 52-54
Wood fill, 76
Wood glue, 21
Workbench, construction of, 29-31
Wrenches, 12